The
RAIKES
Bear & Doll
STORY

by
Linda Mullins

Published by Hobby House Press

Grantsville
Maryland 21536

(Left) Woody Bear Clown. *First Disneyland Convention Bear. 1992. Raikes bear by Applause. 12in (31cm) tall; gray acrylic fur; carved wooden face and foot pads; hand-painted clown face; inset plastic eyes; jointed arms; unjointed floppy legs; swivel head. Dressed in purple and fuchsia clown outfit and hat (colors match painted face). Signed and numbered. Style number 38509. Limited edition of 25. Courtesy Jim and Pam Anderson.*

(Right) Woody Bear Clown. *Disneyland Convention Bear (Second version). 1992. Raikes bear by Applause. 12in (31cm) tall; grey or brown acrylic fur; carved wooden face and foot pads; hand-painted clown face; inset plastic eyes; jointed arms; unjointed floppy legs; swivel head; green and gold clown outfit and rosette (opposed to hat on first version; colors match painted face). Signed and numbered on foot. Style number 38509. Unnumbered. 35 produced to date. Blank certificate. To accommodate disappointed Raikes collectors who attended the 1992 Disneyland convention, but were unable to acquire one of the 25 clown bears produced for the convention, Bob made the decision to have an additional 35 clowns produced. Courtesy Ed and Liz Oerding. Photograph by Ed Oerding.*

Front Cover: *Disneyland 1993 Teddy Bear Classic One-of-a-Kind Auction Piece. Fantasy of the Carousel. Robert Raikes original. Carousel Horse. 24in (61cm) by 24in (61cm); hand-carved wood; hand-painted; inset plastic eyes. Bear. 18in (46cm); black acrylic fur; hand-carved wooden face and foot pads; inset plastic eyes; jointed arms and legs; swivel head. Dressed in cotton print dress with bow at ear. Facade. Hand-carved wooden facade and bear's face; plastic eyes. Action: As music plays horse goes up and down on brass pole and eyes on bear's face move. Courtesy Robert and Carol Raikes.*

Title Page: *Walt Disney World's® 1993 Teddy Bear and Doll Convention One-of-a-Kind Auction Piece. Robert Raikes original. (Left to right) Reindeer. 25in (64cm) tall by 23in (58cm) long; reddish-brown acrylic fur; hand-carved wooden face, antlers and feet; inset plastic eyes; unjointed legs; stationary head.*
Beaver. 15in (38cm) tall; brown acrylic fur; hand-carved wooden face, teeth, paws and feet; inset plastic eyes; jointed arms and legs; swivel head. Dressed in vest and bow tie.
Hedgehog. 13in (33cm) tall; gray acrylic fur; hand-carved wooden face, paws and feet. Dressed in hand-painted tullé with flowers.
Crow. 15in (38cm) tall; black wool fur; hand-carved and hand-painted beak and feet; inset plastic eyes; jointed arms; stationary wings and head.

Elf. 17in (43cm) tall; hand-carved wooden face, hands and soles of shoes; inset plastic eyes; soft stuffed cloth body with poseable wire armature encased in body. Dressed in pants, shirt, leather boots and vest. Hand-carved wooden mandolin.
Mouse. 9in (23cm) tall; hand-carved wooden face; inset plastic eyes; short brown acrylic fur; unjointed body; swivel head.
Bear. 26in (66cm) tall; rust-colored acrylic fur; hand-carved wooden face; foot and paw pads; large inset plastic eyes; jointed arms and legs; swivel head.
Rabbit. 15in (38cm) tall; rust-colored acrylic fur; hand-carved wooden face, paws and foot pads; inset plastic eyes; jointed arms and legs; swivel head. Dressed in pants, shirt and bow tie. Tree. 41in (104cm).
Courtesy Robert and Carol Raikes.

Additional copies of this book may be purchased at $22.95
from
HOBBY HOUSE PRESS, INC.
1 Corporate Drive
Grantsville, Maryland 21536
or from your favorite bookstore or dealer.
Please add $5.50 per copy postage.

© 1991 Linda Mullins
Revised edition © 1993

ISBN: 0-87588-412-1

Table of Contents

Dedication

To Cathy and Robert Raikes Sr., Bob Raikes' wonderful parents.

Introduction

I feel very proud to author this book about Robert Raikes. Since the first time I met him in 1982, I have admired his values and philosophy of life, and his unbelievable talent as an artist and sculptor.

I hope his story of a struggling young artist who worked his way to become one of the most well-known and respected teddy bear artists of the 1980-1990s will inspire other talented artists striving to succeed.

Working in the wood-carving field for nearly two decades, the book reflects on the many hard times Raikes and his family experienced on the long road to success.

Beginning his career hand-carving wooden life-size birds, figures and mantels, Robert Raikes perfected a unique style of wood carving that he not only loved, but he found profitable—creating dolls and teddy bears.

His continued success earned him the recognition as a wood-carver and won him a cherished position in the collectors' world.

Robert Raikes has the gift of blending art and nature, enabling him to express unique personalities in his realistic animal creations.

Unable to meet the increasing demand for his original teddy bears and dolls, Robert Raikes now has a unique association with the well-known gift company, Applause, Inc., to reproduce his original creations. Together they continue to bring the collectors unequaled collectible designs.

Acknowledgements

I wish to thank the following people for making *The Raikes Bear & Doll Story* possible.

My sincere gratitude goes to Bob and Carol Raikes, for allowing me to write the inspiring story of their lives and career.

A special thank you to Cathy and Robert Raikes Sr., Bob's wonderful parents who opened up their home and their hearts to me by sharing personal stories of their son's life, allowing me to photograph their entire collection of his creations and hunting for days to find valuable photographic examples of their son's early work.

My sincerest appreciation to Peter and Janice Spitzer for sharing their extensive collection of Raikes products with me and their vast knowledge of his work.

To Elizabeth Wardley, Marketing Communications Manager at Applause, for her kind cooperation regarding Raikes Creations by Applause.

A great big thank you to my friends, Robert and Pat Woodman and Ed and Liz Oerding, for supplying me with numerous photographs and information on Robert Raikes products by applause.

To my very special friend Georgi Bohrod Rothe, my deepest appreciation for her encouragement and suggestions, and Editor Donna H. Felger for her invaluable advice and patience.

To my publisher, Gary Ruddell, for his support and his faith in me and this book.

Finally, no words can express the gratitude I have for the continued love and tolerance my husband, Wally, has given me.

Chapter One

Robert Raikes Looks Ahead

Robert Raikes goals and plans are best expressed in his own eloquent words.

"When talking about my work I often say that I've created this or that, or I will be creating something in the future. I'm using the word create loosely.

"First of all we are all influenced by others. I'm influenced a great deal by Disney's early work and many artists and sculptors of the past. We all have one thing in common - a need to express ourselves in special ways. However I've learned one real truth, there is only one that creates and that is God. We only mirror His creating, sometimes clearly and sometimes not so clearly. We have all been given gifts of expressing and enjoying that one truth. Unfortunately not all of us understand or want to accept that. I've been blessed with the ability to express a portion of that truth that brings joy to many, satisfaction to myself, not to mention I can feed and support myself and my family.

"Above everything else it is to do the very best work possible. But more specifically there are several areas that I'm concentrating on. First of all for the Raikes bears and animals that all of you know, I'm working to give new life and personality to my work. Most of the large pieces come with a new inset eye that gives a much more life like look as well as more personality. A number of new high quality plushes are being employed to further enhance the look.

"There are a number of new animals that are slowly being introduced through Applause. They include a pig, reindeer, monkey and others.

"Another exciting direction for me and I hope for the collectors of my work, is a wonderful line of fantasy that includes elves, fairies, trolls and other mystical characters. These will be marketed differently than the Applause plush animals. Members of the Robert Raikes Collector's Club (RRCC) will be able to get early information on their progress and how to purchase them.

"Finally, my biggest goal is to reach out and touch more people with my work.

"If I had to describe my personal philosophy in just a few words, it is that I am thankful for the opportunity of being a part of creation. I'm thankful for the awareness of my place in God's creation and I'm thankful that I am able to communicate that through my work. That in a very small and humble way mirrors the beauty and wonderment of God's kingdom for me."

Peter Pan Series. Robert Raikes originals. (Prototypes)

Peter Pan. *1992. 17in (43cm) tall; brown acrylic fur; hand-carved wooden face, foot and paw pads; inset plastic eyes; jointed arms and legs; swivel head. Dressed in green suit and hat; hand-carved knife.*

Captain Hook. *1992. 20in (51cm) tall; black acrylic fur; hand-carved wooden face, beard, hook, paw pad and foot pads; inset plastic eyes; jointed arms and legs; swivel head. Dressed in bright blue pants and hat; blue and burgundy printed jacket and white shirt.*

Wendy. *1993. 18in (46cm) tall; brown acrylic fur; hand-carved wooden face and foot pads; inset "googlie-type" plastic eyes; jointed arms and legs; swivel head. Dressed in a white and blue printed cotton dress; blue bow in hair.*

Johnathon. *1993. 12in (31cm) tall; light brown acrylic fur; hand-carved wooden face; foot and paw pads; inset plastic eyes; jointed arms and legs; swivel head. Dressed in pale blue night suit and cap.*

Tinkerbell. *1992. 7in (18cm) tall; pale green acrylic plush; hand-carved wooden face and foot pads; inset plastic eyes; jointed arms and legs; swivel head. Dressed in pale pink petal skirt and white lace top; pink net wings.*

Crocodile. *1993. 17in (43cm) tall by 20in (51cm) long; bright green sequin material body; hand-carved wooden face, feet and paws; hand-painted eyes. The ship was made by Bob's son Jason. Courtesy Robert and Carol Raikes.*

(Left) Boy doll. Robert Raikes original (Prototype). 1989. 13in (33cm) tall; hand-carved wooden face, hair, hands and feet; soft-stuffed cloth bodies; poseable wire armature encased in body. Dressed in navy blue pants, brown tweed jacket, white shirt and tie. Courtesy Robert and Carol Raikes.

(Right) Girl doll. Robert Raikes original (Prototype). 1989. 13in (33cm) tall; hand-carved wooden face, hair, hands and feet; soft-stuffed cloth bodies; poseable wire armature encased in body. Dressed in white cotton dress.

(Left) Storyteller. Robert Raikes original (Prototype). 1991. 20in (51cm); hand-carved wooden face, beard, eyebrows, hands and soles of shoes; soft-stuffed body with poseable wire armature encased in body. Dressed in wool pants, vest, shawl and beige cotton shirt. Carrying a hand-carved wooden staff and pouch strapped across body. Courtesy Bob and Carol Raikes.

(Right) Flower Fairy. Robert Raikes original (Prototype). 1992. 9in (23cm); white acrylic fur; hand-carved wooden face; inset plastic eyes; jointed arms and legs; swivel head. Dressed in pink shell skirt, white net wings, flower in hair.

Baker. Storybook Series. Robert Raikes original (Prototype). 1993. 13in (33cm) tall; black acrylic fur; hand-carved wooden face and foot pads; inset plastic "googlie-type" eyes; jointed arms and legs; swivel head. Dressed in white apron and cap with red and white striped shirt. Courtesy Robert and Carol Raikes.

OPPOSITE PAGE: Little Miss Muffett. Storybook Series. Robert Raikes original (Prototype). 1993. 13in (33cm) tall; cream-colored acrylic fur; hand-carved wooden face and foot pads; inset plastic "googlie-type" eyes; jointed arms and legs; swivel head. Dressed in pink taffeta dress with matching bow at ear. Dress trimmed with white lace. Courtesy Robert and Carol Raikes.

OPPOSITE PAGE INSET: (Left) Elf. Robert Raikes original (Prototype). 1993. 14in (36cm) tall; white acrylic fur; hand-carved wooden face and foot pads; inset plastic eyes; jointed arms and legs; swivel head. Dressed in green net skirt trimmed with pink, net rosette at ear and white net wings.

(Center left) Gnome Groom. Robert Raikes original (Prototype). 1993. 17in (43cm); hand-carved wooden face and hands; large inset plastic eyes; soft-stuffed body with poseable wire armature encased in body. Dressed in white shirt, gray pants and shoes with hand-carved wooden soles.

(Center right) Gnome Bride. Robert Raikes original (Prototype). 1993. 17in (43cm); hand-carved wooden face and hands; large inset plastic eyes; soft-stuffed body with poseable wire armature encased in body. Dressed in white silk long wedding dress with white net veil and shoes with hand-carved wooden soles.

(Right) Elf. Robert Raikes original (Prototype). 1993. 14in (36cm) tall; white acrylic fur; hand-carved wooden face and foot pads; inset plastic eyes; jointed arms and legs; swivel head. Dressed in bright fuchsia net skirt with net rosette at ear and white net wings.

Courtesy Robert and Carol Raikes.

Little Pig Went to Market. Storybook Series. Robert Raikes original (Prototype). 1993. 14in (36cm) tall; pink acrylic fur; hand-carved wooden face, paws and feet; inset plastic "googlie-type" eyes; jointed arms and legs; swivel head. Dressed in blue velveteen suit, white shirt and floral bow tie. Courtesy Robert and Carol Raikes.

Pilgrim Lady, *a beautiful Raikes original was philanthropically donated as an auction item to benefit the Plymouth Plantation.*

The agricultural center at the Massachusetts historical site was devastated by a fire which swept through the complex and destroyed 77 animals.

Avid Raikes collectors, Ed and Liz Oerding from Oregon, purchased the Raikes donation (January 1993) which contributed valuable funds needed to acquire new animals and rebuild the rare animal breeding program which played an important role in depicting life in the early 17th Century.

Jack. *Storybook Series. Robert Raikes original (Prototype). 1993. 13in (33cm) tall; caramel-colored acrylic fur; hand-carved wooden face and foot pads; inset plastic "googlie-type" eyes; jointed arms and legs; swivel head. Dressed in brown check pants and floral blouse.* Courtesy Robert and Carol Raikes.

Georgy Porgy. *Storybook Series. Robert Raikes original (Prototype). 1993. 13in (33cm) tall; brown colored acrylic fur; hand-carved wooden face and foot pads; inset plastic "googlie-type" eyes; jointed arms and legs; swivel head. Dressed in blue suit, red and black striped vest, white shirt and large red bow tie.* Courtesy Robert and Carol Raikes.

Bear. *Robert Raikes original (Prototype). 1992. 18in (46cm) tall; black acrylic fur; hand-carved wooden face and foot pads; inset plastic "googlie-type" eyes; jointed arms and legs; swivel head. Note: new facial design.* Courtesy Robert and Carol Raikes.

Chapter Two

Robert Raikes Collector's Club & Disney Conventions

Raikes' bears popularity has snowballed over the years. Much of the stimulus to the increasing value and enthusiasm of these creative creatures can be attributed to the Robert Raikes Collector's Club (RRCC), Convention and Special Disney Conventions.

Robert Raikes Collector's Club

Robert Raikes began the RRCC in 1988. His goal, to make this club a "special experience" for all club members, has been achieved. Today the club numbers more than 6000 members! Each member receives a membership bear, a membership card, a quarterly newsletter ("Bear Facts"), monthly messages via a designated access number, chances to win original creations or monthly drawings <u>and</u> the exclusive opportunity to purchase special limited editions for Club members only.

These limited "Club Editions" have so far included black *Terry* (similar to the 12in white and brown *Terry* release to the public in 1988), the *Panda* (noted for the difficulty in producing its white face) and *Tammy*. Other pieces such as AP (Artist Proof) *Nicolette* and *Francie* have only been offered to members.

Whereas *Terry*, *Panda* and *Tammy* were produced in lots of approximately 4000 (with a few returned by the club to Applause as defective), only 300 AP *Nicolettes* were produced. *Francie* only numbered 1000 total production.

Nicolette was hand-signed and *Francie* comes with a hand-signed certificate.

These bears are even difficult for club members to purchase due to the limited production runs.

Robert Raikes Collector's Club Convention

One truly unique component of the RRCC is the annual convention. Each event takes the hard work of the Raikes family, Marilyn Santos (Bob's assistant) and dedicated volunteers. An innovative theme or promotion is also an integral facet of the yearly gatherings. The convention also features speakers, bear signing and the opportunity for RRCC members to meet their hero, Robert Raikes, in person. According to RRCC literature, "they are always amazed as what a down to earth person he is. And ... Bob is always impressed with how warm and friendly his collectors are."

First Robert Raikes Collector's Club Convention: "Pirates of the Pacific"
Date: October 13-15, 1989
Place: Woodland Hills, California
Coordinators: A.B.C. Unlimited Productions
Convention Bears: *M'Lady Honeypot* and *Billy Buccaneer* (sold as a pair). Limited edition of 2500 (sets).
Highlights of event:

The response to the first Robert Raikes Collector's Club Convention was overwhelming. Open to club members only, the theme of this successful event was "Pirates of the Pacific."

Conventioneers toured Applause (located in Woodland Hills), after Bob gave a wood-carving demonstration with everyone invited to participate in a workshop. Under the supervision of the celebrity carver himself, the students attempted their own versions of a Raikes bear face.

Former Applause Vice-President, Gary Trumbo, entertained the gathering by recalling the notable, business, personal and humorous events he had shared with the sculptor.

Former Applause Product Manager, Joe Dumbacher, gave an informative slide presentation on Raikes' creations produced by Applause. Robert Woodman, avid Raikes collector and historian, gave a magnificent slide presentation of his collection of Bob's original work.

Bob poses for a picture at a 1991 signing with one of his young fans. Jeremy Knobel loves Raikes bears especially the one he affectionately holds as they bear the same name — Jeremy. Courtesy Toba S. Knobel.

Clown (Prototype). Robert Raikes original. 1992. Special Edition bear for Robert Raikes Collector's Club members. Proposed release 1994 in an edition of 500. Courtesy Ed and Liz Oerding. Photograph by Ed Oerding.

Bob Raikes takes a few moments to relax from his busy schedule at his second Robert Raikes Collector's Club Convention in Nashville, Tennessee in September 1990 to visit with his friend, Raikes collector and dealer Ed Oerding. Courtesy Ed and Liz Oerding. Photograph by Ed Oerding.

Members of Bob's family and business associates posed for this group photograph at the Fourth Annual Robert Raikes Collector's Club Convention in Seattle, Washington, held July 31 through August 2, 1992. Left to right are Pat Carless, Bob's seamstress; Marilyn Santos, RRCC administrator; Vern Santos, Marilyn's husband; Carol Raikes, Bob's wife; Emily Raikes, Bob's youngest daughter; Catherine Raikes, Bob's mother; Victoria Connell, RRCC member from Australia. Courtesy Marilyn Santos.

Author Linda Mullins autographs her newly released book The Raikes Bear & Doll Story (First Edition) at a teddy bear event in October, 1991. Courtesy Ed and Liz Oerding. Photograph by Ed Oerding.

Robert Raikes' children (Emily [left] and Jenny [right]) had fun posing for this photograph at the Fourth Annual Robert Raikes Collector's Club Convention in Seattle, Washington. The bear was SO LARGE it had to be shipped to Washington from Arizona in five separate boxes.

Upon arrival the bear was assembled. This one-of-a-kind masterpiece is fully jointed with large wooden discs secured with nuts and bolts. Sixty-five pounds of stuffing was used to fill the body cavity. Courtesy Bob and Carol Raikes.

Second Robert Raikes Collector's Club Convention: "Calico Pete At The Grand Ole Opry"
Date: September 13-16, 1990
Place: Nashville, Tennessee
Coordinators: A.B.C. Unlimited Productions
Convention Bear: *Calico Pete*. Limited edition of 1500.
Highlights of event:

A lively dialog between speakers Bob Raikes, Marilyn Santos, Applause's Joe Dumbacher and the audience marked the onset of the convention. A Saturday seminar featured Joe Dumbacher's address illustrating the step-by-step production process of *Calico Pete*. The annual workshop project was the building of a wooden chuck wagon model kit. A charity auction raised $50,000 for the Christian Children's Fund, Easter Seals, National Youth Ministry and Good Bears of the World. Nearly three dozen original pieces and Applause prototypes were auctioned off.

Third Robert Raikes Collector's Club Convention: "Tropical Fantasy"
Date: May 18-25, 1991
Place: A Caribbean Cruise aboard the Sovereign of the Seas, the Royal Caribbean's cruise ship
Coordinators: A.B.C. Unlimited Productions
Convention Bear: *Savanna*. Limited edition of 1000.
Highlights of event:

Perhaps the most significant highlight of the third convention was the unique creation of *Savanna*, a 9in (23cm) tall, wood and elastic cord jointed commemorative limited edition piece. Raikes has been using elastic cord since 1984 on his original dolls and incorporated its utilization in this unusual piece.

The Joe Dumbacher seminar provided collectors a review of new Raikes pieces and an overview of the production techniques employed in the making of *Savanna*.

Five originals were sold at a silent auction. The proceeds were donated to a Mexican Christian community to which Bob is teaching the art of quilting.

Fourth Robert Raikes Collector's Club Convention:
Date: July 31-August 2, 1992
Place: Seattle, Washington
Coordinators: Robert Raikes and Marilyn Santos
Convention Bear: *Petunia*. Limited edition of 250.
Highlights of event:

Robert Raikes created a 9ft (273cm)tall bear so large that it needed to be transported in several pieces. Final assembly took place only hours before the event and included stuffing the creature with 70 pounds of material. Seminars were held by Leslie Gross (Former Vice President of Product Development) and Alison Rodnon (Product Manager) of Applause. This year's auction of 22 originals netted $36,800.

(Left) Panda. *Robert Raikes Collector's Club Raikes Bear. Second edition. 1990. Raikes Panda by Applause. 11in (28cm) tall; black and white acrylic fur; hand-painted black and white carved wooden face and foot pads; inset plastic eyes; jointed arms and legs; swivel head; signed and numbered on foot. Style number 30303. 4000 produced.*
(Center) Tammy. *Robert Raikes Collector's Club Bear. Third edition. 1992. Raikes bear by Applause. 7in (18cm) tall; brown acrylic fur; carved wooden face and foot pads; inset plastic eyes; jointed arms and legs; swivel head; signed and numbered on foot. Style number 30375. 4000 produced, Dressed in white cotton dress trimmed with lace. Red bow on dress and red bow with lace trim affixed to ear.*
(Right) Terry. *Robert Raikes Collector's Club Bear. First edition. 1988. Raikes bear by Applause. 12in (31cm) tall; black acrylic fur; carved wooden face and foot pads; inset plastic eyes; jointed arms and legs; swivel head; signed and numbered on foot. Style number 17010. 4000 produced.*
Courtesy Ed and Liz Oerding. Photograph by Ed Oerding.

M'Lady Honeypot *and* Billy Buccaneer. *First Robert Raikes Collector's Club Convention Bears, "Pirates of the Pacific". 1989. Raikes bears by The Good Company.*
(Left) M'Lady Honeypot. *12in (31cm) tall; dark brown acrylic fur; carved wooden face and foot pads; inset plastic eyes; jointed arms and legs; swivel head; signed and numbered on foot. Style number 30178. Dressed in black skirt and hat and gold satin blouse.*
(Right) Billy Buccaneer. *12in (31cm) tall; dark brown acrylic fur; carved wooden face, foot pad and peg leg; inset plastic eyes; jointed arms and legs; swivel head; signed and numbered on foot; style number 30178. Dressed as a pirate in a black velvet coat, colorful bandana and a black patch over one eye. Sold as a pair. Limited edition of 2500. Both bears come with identical numbers and share one certificate and specially designed "Pirates of the Pacific" box.*

(Left) Calico Pete. *Second Robert Raikes Collector's Convention Edition. 1990. Raikes bear by Applause. 17in (43cm) tall; brown acrylic fur; carved wooden face and boots (boots are hand-painted with silver tips); inset plastic eyes; unjointed arms and legs; stationary head. Dressed in black suit with silver buckle; holds black felt hat. Carved wooden guitar, fence and saddle. Colorful blanket draped over fence; nylon rope lasso hangs on saddle. Bear and fence mounted on base. Signed and numbered. Style number 30304. Limited edition of 1500.*
(Right) Savanna. *Third Annual Robert Raikes Convention Edition. "Tropical Fantasy." 1991. Raikes bear by Applause. 10in (25cm) tall; carved wooden head and body; inset plastic eyes; jointed arms and legs; swivel head. Dressed in native Caribbean outfit, accented by beaded necklace, ankle bracelet and hoop earrings. Signed and numbered. Style number 30324. Limited edition of 1000.*
Courtesy Ed and Liz Oerding. Photograph by Ed Oerding.

Fifth Robert Raikes Collector's Club Convention:
Date: October 22 - 24, 1993
Place: Lancaster, Pennsylvania
Coordinators: Robert Raikes and Marilyn Santos
Convention Bears: *Jacob* and *Katie* (sold as a pair). Limited edition of 500 (sets).
Highlights of event:
   The annual theme included a tour of an Amish farm and house, a ride on the Strasburg Railroad and a stop at the Kitchen Kettle Village.

Walt Disney World® and Disneyland Conventions
   A relatively new teddy bear event which has proved to be extremely successful is the Walt Disney World® Teddy Bear and Doll Convention in Orlando, Florida. Amid the fireworks and performances, this gala event includes the sale of limited edition bears and parkwide exhibits, displays and demonstrations by bear artists and manufacturers. A one-of-a-kind auction is held for conventioneers only.
   Bob Raikes is one of the most popular draws at the Disney conventions. He has provided limited editions of up to 500.
   The large following of fans makes Robert Raikes and his work valuable to the Disney organization when putting together one of its shows.
   Bill Davidson, one of the main buyers for Walt Disney World® in Florida, spoke highly of Robert Raikes and his work. His testimonial appearing in The Bugle (now Raikes Review) best says it all:
   "I think for Robert's medium, it's exceptional. He puts life into a piece of wood like I've never seen anyone else put into it. That life is then transcribed into what Applause does, which is very important. He has his own character that he puts into his work. People feel that they are getting something really different and really magical — and they are."

Second Walt Disney World® Teddy Bear and Doll Convention 1989.
First Limited Edition Convention Bear: *Terry* bear (black)
   Raikes' first appearance at a Disney show was actually in 1988, but it wasn't until the second Walt Disney World® Convention that a limited edition was available. One hundred *Black Terry* bears were attired in Disney Convention T-shirts and a "wooden balloon with ears" hand-signed by the artist was affixed to the arm. Each numbered toy was priced at $135. Purchasers also received a Club membership and the Disney bear also acted as that new member's Club bear.
Auction Bear: A 5ft original Raikes bear dressed in a Disney T-shirt brought nearly $4,000 at auction.

Third Walt Disney World® Teddy Bear and Doll Convention 1990.
Second Limited Edition Convention Bear: *Dolly and Her Rocking Horse*
   Raikes' early interest in carousel horses inspired this limited edition which sold for $195. It came boxed with a certificate. This totally new miniature was produced exclusively for the Disney Convention in an edition of 500.
Auction Bears: *Hans* and *Gretchen* ("The Swiss Bears")
   "The Swiss Bears" (30in [76cm] height) similar to the Alpine pieces auctioned at the RRCC in Tennessee, netted more than $5,500 in auction. The boy, *Hans*, wears lederhosen and the girl, *Gretchen*, the traditional dirndl skirt.

Petunia. *Fourth Robert Raikes Collector's Convention Edition. 1992. Raikes bear by Applause. 20in (51cm) tall; cream-colored acrylic fur; carved wooden face and foot pads; inset plastic eyes; jointed arms and legs; swivel head. Dressed in calico print dress with lace trim, white eyelet apron and straw hat. She carries a wicker picnic basket. Signed and numbered. Style number 30643. Limited edition of 250. Note long snout and smooth foot pads, features not produced since first edition Rebecca in 1985.*
Courtesy Bob and Pat Woodman. Photograph by Robert Woodman.

Jacob *and* Katie. *Fifth Robert Raikes Collector's Convention Edition. 1993. Raikes bears by Applause. 18in (46cm) tall;*
(Left) Katie. *Dark brown acrylic fur; carved wooden face and foot pads; inset plastic eyes; jointed arms and legs; swivel head. Dressed in blue dress with white shawl and bonnet, carrying a basket. Style number N/A.*
(Right) Jacob. *Dark brown acrylic fur; carved wooden face, beard and foot pads; inset plastic eyes; jointed arms and legs; swivel head. Dressed in black pants and hat with white shirt, holding a wooden walking stick. Style number N/A. Limited edition of 500 sets.* Courtesy Robert and Carol Raikes.

Nicolettes. *(Right) Artist Proof. Fourth Christmas Edition. 1991. Raikes bears by Applause. 16in (41cm) tall; brown acrylic fur; carved wooden faces and foot pads; inset plastic eyes; jointed arms and legs; swivel heads. Dressed in a red dress with a green Christmas tree print with matching bonnet. Carrying a green Christmas stocking with cotton eyelet trim. Artist Proof Nicolette has embroidered on trim an appliqued Christmas tree. Signed and numbered. Style number 51243. General limited edition of 10,000. Artist Proof 300 (designated AP on paw). The Artist Proof edition was reserved and hand signed by Robert Raikes exclusively for the Robert Raikes Collector's Club members. Each comes with a certificate and special registration. Style number 38567.*
Courtesy Robert and Pat Woodman. Photograph by Robert Woodman.

Francie. *Robert Raikes Collector's Club Special Edition. 1992. Raikes bear by Applause. 14in (36cm) tall; honey-colored acrylic fur; carved wooden face and foot pads; inset plastic eyes; jointed arms and legs; swivel head. Dressed in pink and white checked gingham dress with a white satin ribbon around her waist and a pink checked headband. Accompanied by a white painted wooden duck pull toy with yellow painted wheels. Style number 30271. Limited edition of 1000. Note unique feature hand-numbered in black ink.* Courtesy Robert and Pat Woodman. Photograph by Robert Woodman.

Robert Raikes takes a few minutes to pose for a picture during his signing session at the 1991 Walt Disney World® Teddy Bear Convention with Raikes collector and dealer Liz Oerding. Note in the background waiting to be adopted are the Raikes Kris Kringle bears produced in an edition of 500 especially for the convention. Courtesy Ed and Liz Oerding. Photograph by Ed Oerding.

Terry Bear. *First edition Walt Disney World® Piece 1989. Raikes bear by Applause. 12in (31cm) tall; black acrylic fur; carved wooden face and foot pads; inset plastic eyes; jointed arms and legs; swivel head; signed on foot. Wearing a Walt Disney World® 1989 Teddy Bear Convention T-shirt, holding three balloons. Limited edition of 100. Each bear came with a Robert Raikes Collector's Club membership.* Courtesy Robert and Pat Woodman. Photograph by Robert Woodman.

Walt Disney World's® 1991 Teddy Bear and Doll Convention One-of-a-Kind Auction Piece. Gerbeardi and Zuzu. Robert Raikes Originals. Bringing the fantastic sum of $10,000, this appealing classic Raikes original bear has a hand-carved mahogany face with a handlebar mustache. Animated by Robert Raikes, Senior, music can be heard as the bear cranks the hurdy gurdy while his baby monkey Zuzu sits atop the organ sucking his wooden thumb. Courtesy Robert and Carol Raikes.

Fourth Walt Disney World® Teddy Bear and Doll Convention 1991
Third Limited Edition Convention Bear: *Kris Kringle*

The holiday season influenced the creation of *Kris Kringle*, a 12in (31cm) Savanna-type all wood bear with a musical bag. In all, 500 of this edition were released and sold for $185. The combination of limited edition bear sales and auction price made Raikes the top selling bear artist at the show.

Auction Bear and Monkey: *Gerbeardi* and *Zuzu*

A bidder from California paid $10,000 over the phone for this mechanical work of art. Robert Raikes, Sr. insured that the bear was mechanical, moving its forearm to power an old time organ. The organ grinder, *Gerbeardi*, has a hand-carved mahogany face with handlebar mustache. *Zuzu*, his baby monkey, perches on the decorated hand organ and sucks his thumb.

Fifth Walt Disney World® Teddy Bear and Doll Convention 1992
Fourth Limited Edition Convention Bear: *Mary Had a Little Lamb*

This appealing nursery rhyme character stole the hearts of Raikes collectors and even at $225 the 250 edition sold out in three days. Disney marketing representatives reported they received hundreds of phone calls from collectors hoping to be able to order this special bear.

Auction Piece: *Barber Shop Quartet*

A quartet of hand-carved pieces ranging in size from 18in (46cm) to 42in (107cm), crafted in a rich brown mohair, these bears appear in a setting with a barber chair and many barber poles. Sitting in a barber's chair, a pouting bear (*Antonio* — 18in [46cm]) watches the singers *Luigi* (38in [96cm]), *Guiseppi* (34in [86cm]), *Alfredo* (37in [94cm]) and *Saracco* (42in [107cm]). At a realized price of $9250, this one-of-a-kind appealing scene was the highest price piece in the auction.

Walt Disney World's® 1990 Teddy Bear and Doll Convention One-of-a-Kind Auction Piece. Hans *and* Gretchen *("The Swiss Bears")*. Robert Raikes originals. 30in (76cm) tall; dark brown acrylic fur; hand-carved wooden faces and paw pads; inset plastic eyes; jointed arms and legs; swivel head. Hans *is dressed in classic lederhosen and* Gretchen *wears the traditional dirndl dress.* Courtesy Applause.

(*Left*) Dolly on Her Rocking Horse. *Second edition Walt Disney World® Piece.* 1990. Raikes bear and horse by Applause. Dolly. 8in (20cm) tall; light brown acrylic fur; carved wooden face and foot pads; inset plastic eyes; stationary arms; jointed legs; swivel head; signed and

numbered on foot. Rocking Horse. 9in (23cm) tall; by 13in (33cm) long; hand-carved wood; hand-painted eyes; mane, tail and blanket; leather reins. Signed and numbered on foot. Style number 40259. Limited edition of 500 sets.

(*Right*) Kris Kringle. *Third edition Walt Disney World® Convention bear.* 1991. Raikes bear by Applause. 12in (31cm) tall; all wood hand-carved head and body; jointed (with nylon cord) arms and legs; swivel head; inset plastic eyes; white acrylic fur beard (pull down [not permanently attached]); dressed in traditional red and white Santa outfit; green bag encases music box (plays "Jingle Bells"). Signed and numbered on foot. Style number 40304. Limited edition of 500. Courtesy Ed and Liz Oerding. Photograph by Ed Oerding.

First Disneyland Teddy Bear Classic 1992
Limited Edition Convention Bear: *Disney Clown*

Using 12in (31cm) Applause Woody bears, each *Disney Clown* sported a clown face painted in purple, aqua and gold. Their costume was a purple and fuchsia lamé clown costume, complete with pointy hat. Called the Jester bear by Disney officials, the limited edition of 25 was priced at $125. Again, Raikes was number one in show sales.
Auction Piece: *At the Circus*

Vicki Todd purchased the Raikes piece *At the Circus* for $11,000. The five original creations and their colorful musical animated environment are on display at Vicki's Gifts and Collectibles in West Hills, California.

Second Disneyland Teddy Bear and Doll Classic 1993
Limited Edition Convention Bear: *Millie*

There were only eight Raikes bears produced for this year's limited edition. However, these special bears were all personally hand-carved by the artist specifically for the event. Complete with butter churn, *Millie* is dressed to represent a pioneer lady from the 1800s. Retailing for $1250 each, one of these bears resold shortly after the event for $3000.
Auction Piece: *Fantasy of the Carousel*

The 24in (61cm) jeweled hand-carved horse moves up and down to the magical sound of the carousel music, encased within this attractive setting. The recognizable face of a Raikes bear's head with moveable eyes, decorates the facade. Proudly seated enjoying the ride is *Mandy*, an 18in (46cm) bear. This incredible one-of-a-kind Raikes original piece brought $8600. Marilyn's World of Lauderhill, Florida, is the happy owner of this magnificent piece.

Mary Had A Little Lamb. *Fourth edition Walt Disney World® Convention Piece.* 1992. Mary. Raikes bear by Applause. 19in (48cm) tall; beige acrylic fur; dark mahogany carved wooden face and foot pads; inset plastic eyes; jointed arms and legs; swivel head. Dressed in a mauve cotton printed dress with white pinafore embroidered with flowers. Signed and numbered on foot. Style number 60050. Lamb. Raikes lamb by Applause. 7in (18cm) tall by 9in (3cm) long; white fleece; carved wooden face; pink cotton feet; inset blue plastic eyes; unjointed arms and legs; stationary head. Pink ribbon tied around neck. Limited edition of 250. Courtesy Ed and Liz Oerding. Photograph by Ed Oerding.

Disneyland 1992 Teddy Bear Classic One-of-a-Kind Auction Piece. At the Circus. Robert Raikes original. Five fascinating animals create the colorful musical animated environment. Lion. *21½in (55cm) tall; gold acrylic fur; hand-carved wooden face; inset plastic eyes.* Ringmaster Bear. *37½in (95cm) tall (including hat); brown mohair; hand-carved wooden (mahogany) face and paw pads; inset plastic eyes.* Monkey. *14in (36cm) tall; brown acrylic fur; hand-carved wooden face and paws; inset plastic eyes.* Bear (riding unicycle). *32½in (83cm) tall; white acrylic fur; hand-carved face and paw pads; hand-painted face; inset plastic eyes.* Jester Bear. *14in (36cm) tall; pale beige acrylic fur; hand-carved wooden face and paw pads; inset plastic eyes. Holding cotton candy.* Courtesy Vicki's Gifts and Collectibles. Photograph by James Stader.

Walt Disney World's® 1992 Teddy Bear and Doll Convention. One-of-a-Kind Auction Piece. Barber Shop Quartet. A Robert Raikes original. A quartet of hand-carved pieces ranging in size from 18in (46cm) to 42in (107cm). Crafted in rich brown mohair, these bears appear in a setting with a barber chair and many barber poles. Sitting in a barber's chair, a pouting bear (Antonio — 18in [46cm]) watches the singers Luigi (38in [96cm]), Guiseppi (34in [86cm]), Alfredo (37in [94cm]) and Saracco (42in [107cm]). Bob Raikes proudly poses beside his creation with an old school friend. Courtesy Robert and Carol Raikes.

Millie. *Second edition. Disneyland's Convention bear. 1993. Robert Raikes original. 28in (71cm) tall; dark brown acrylic fur; hand-carved mahogany wooden face and foot pads; inset plastic eyes; jointed arms and legs; swivel head; dressed as a pioneer lady with butter churn. Signed and numbered on foot. (#1 of 8).* Courtesy Gary Silber (Bear Tracker, Inc.).

Chapter Three

The Life of Robert Raikes

The Raikes bear story is of a young artist who conceived the idea of creating teddy bears with hand-carved wooden faces. Over the years, Robert Raikes worked his way to become one of the most famous teddy bear artists in the history of the craft.

Born on October 13, 1947, in Van Nuys, California, Bob Raikes was the oldest son among the three children of Robert and Cathy Raikes. As his father's work caused them to move about frequently, Bob traveled considerably as a child. The family even lived in England for a year.

Bob had no formal art education or training. He feels he inherited his talent of drawing from his father, who was a cartoonist. Bob recalls that the first carving he ever did was in junior high school, when he carved the face of his friend on a small piece of wood and presented it to her on a church camping trip. He does not remember carving again until 1969.

He was serving three years in the United States Navy and was stationed in southeast Asia. He carved the word "love" on a block of wood he found on the Navy base and mailed it to his teenage sweetheart, Carol, who was later to become his wife. This early representation of Bob's work is Carol's most cherished possession.

In 1970, when Bob was discharged from the service, he married Carol. In 1973, he enrolled as a student at the California Polytechnical College. During the summer break at the college, he met Gilbert Valencia, the chief carver for the Wetherby Rifle Company. Valencia was also noted for his religious carvings. Bob was fascinated by the elderly Mexican's carvings.

Bob and Carol Raikes with their young son, Jason.
Courtesy of Cathy and Robert Raikes Sr.

This early photo of Bob carving shows Bob's son Jason totally engrossed in watching his father take a plain piece of wood and in no time at all transform it into an ornately carved placque. Courtesy of Bob and Carol Raikes.

Valencia allowed Bob to watch him on a regular basis. "I think he thought I was only going to last a couple of days," Bob recalls. "But those days turned into months. After he saw that I was serious about carving, he let me use his tools, something he had never let anybody else do."

By the end of the summer, Bob had purchased his own tools and began to create his own style of carving. "I fumbled around with it for several years," he said of the wood sculpting.

As an enthusiastic artist, he joined the National Carvers Association and obtained a job teaching carving at Adult Education classes and local high schools. He began specializing in life-size birds and won an award for the best novice carver.

Bob loved what he was doing and after serious thought, he asked his wife, Carol, to keep her job as a dental assistant full-time for two years, allowing him to develop his new skills. His goal was to turn his hobby into a full-time profession. Bob worked 12 to 16 hours a day, carving everything from mantels and headboards, to figures and animals.

In 1974, Bob's and Carol's first child, Jason, was born. One of the highlights of those early days was the sale of one of Bob's life-size eagles for $3500. In the little coastal town of Morro Bay, California, where the Raikes family lived for awhile, Bob was commissioned to carve a life-sized pelican, by Hofbrauer Restaurant, located on the Embarcadero.

I was thrilled to see this fine piece of workmanship when I visited Morro Bay in 1988. Morro Bay is now a popular resort town and Bob's pelican is enjoyed by thousands of tourists each year. Proudly standing with its wings lifted, ready for flight, it is a beautiful sight as it is silhouetted against the colorful sunsets. Examples of Bob's early work are visible all over the little beach town. Bob's attractive hand-carved wooden signs greeted my husband and me on the outside of many of the quaint shops.

Then, one day in 1975, an admirer of Bob's work asked him to make some carved wooden dolls. "They turned out rather folksy-looking," said Bob. The heads were wood, with sawdust-filled cloth bodies. But everyone appeared to like them. Since this was a new area for Bob, he was a little apprehensive to just concentrate on doll making. So, he kept carving his animals.

Bob asked Carol to continue working for another year, giving him one more year to try to make it as a carver. According to Bob, it was a do-or-die situation.

The cost of living was so high where the young couple lived that in 1978, they eagerly started a new life by purchasing five acres of their own land in the mountains of Grass Valley, California. Bob's dream was always to work among the trees and to breathe clean air. He felt this peaceful setting would allow him to really concentrate on his carving.

Bob still worked hard at his carving, cutting down his own trees and curing the lumber. He did well selling his carvings at craft shows and through his parents' antique shop in San Luis Obispo, California. But it seemed as hard as he worked, the young couple could not get ahead. Even the weather was against them. Their first winter in the mountains was the worst winter in Grass Valley in 30 years. The snow climbed above the windows of their little trailer. In 1978, when their second child, Jenny, was born, the couple decided the living conditions would be too hard on the new baby, so they left their beautiful mountains and moved back into town.

They moved frequently in the next few years in an attempt to outrun the spreading inflation. "We actually ran out of places to turn," Bob said. For extra money, he did odd jobs, yard work, picked apples, refinished furniture. Carol encouraged him all the way. Eventually, the couple decided to rent a home in Mount Shasta, California. As wood has always been Bob's focal point, he felt he would achieve his best work among the trees and mountains, an environment he found inspirational.

Between 1974 and 1976, Bob carved approximately a dozen miniature carousel horses. In 1975, he formed two half-scale models. However, it was Bob's grand life-size carousel horses that generated much attention during his earlier days. In 1981, he designed two magnificently carved carousel horses for the Holiday Inn in Santa Margarita, California. These gaily painted works of art were used as part of the inn's carousel.

These early carousel horses sing with a tune all their own. The process for these colorful creatures takes a month. It begins with design work and after a full-scale sketch of the horse is finished, Raikes planes and glues the wood. The work must be perfect and can become quite tedious. A band saw cuts sections of wood and the pieces are glued together.

Then comes the sanding, by far the most time-consuming activity. Finally, Raikes constructs a "hollow box" for the body, carefully adding legs, head and tail with precision and care, one piece at a time. Once the body is completed, the horses are lacquered and painted.

Pelican. 1974. A Robert Raikes original, all hand-carved driftwood.

Robert Raikes was commissioned to carve this life-size pelican by the Hofbrau Restaurant located on the waterfront at Morro Bay, California. This fine example of Bob's work is enjoyed by thousands of tourists each year. Proudly standing with his wings lifted, ready for flight, it is a beautiful sight as it is silhouetted against the colorful sunsets. Courtesy of Hofbrau Restaurant, Morro Bay, California.

Robert Raikes began hand-carving life-size birds early in his career. This magnificent and very difficult carving, Gulls in the Breeze, *was created from a large alder driftwood stump in 1975. Approximate size, 72in (213cm) tall.* Courtesy of Robert and Carol Raikes.

Carved Face. 1975. A Robert Raikes original. 14in (36cm) tall; all hand-carved wood.

One-of-a-kind. An ancient wooden mask was the inspiration for this fine example of Raikes' early carvings. Courtesy of Robert and Carol Raikes.

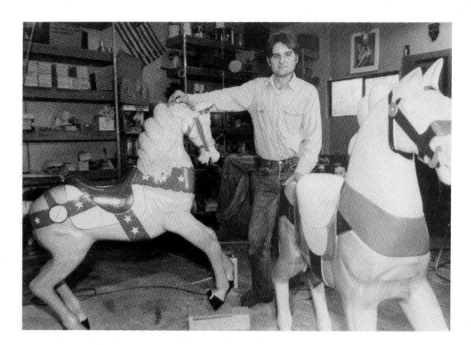

Life-size Carousel Horses. 1981. Robert Raikes originals; all hand-carved wood.

Robert Raikes stands with two of his carousel horses that were destined for the Holiday Inn in Santa Margarita, California. These gaily painted works of art were part of the Inn's carousel. Courtesy of The Mount Shasta Herald.

Robert Raikes Sr. proudly stands by one of his son's magnificently carved life-size carousel horses. Courtesy of Pizazz Antiques, Morro Bay, California.

Robert Raikes won the award for the best novice carver when he entered his life-size barn owl in the "Fly Away" contest in 1981. Raikes intricately hand-carved this realistic-looking bird in 1977. Courtesy of Robert and Carol Raikes.

When the finished work is over, Raikes faces the problem of shipping. Once, one horse arrived in Arizona with two broken legs. (The tail is removeable so at least that appendage arrived intact.)

As more and more people requested his dolls, he decided to put all his efforts into just making dolls. Bob felt these were more lucrative and the new area was a challenge to him.

As always, Carol supported his efforts. She now worked right along Bob, making clothes and bodies for the dolls. Miraculously, things began to improve for the struggling young artist who, up until this time, had spent most of his married life just trying to pay the bills.

Nervously, Bob and Carol Raikes exhibited at their first doll show in 1981. It was a small event in Santa Rosa, California, that really featured miniatures. Bob designed approximately 20 miniature dolls especially for the event. These were the only miniature dolls he remembers making. The apprehensive couple's fears were soon overcome by the response of the collectors at the show. By the end of the day, they were overwhelmed by their total doll sales of $800. Seeing the potential at the doll shows, they decided to exhibit at a major event in Anaheim, California.

The enthusiastic couple worked night and day and made a total of 32 dolls in three months. As the Anaheim show was a long distance for the couple to travel with their two small children, Bob's parents, who lived closer to the event, offered to work the show for them. As an added attraction, the senior Raikes created a miniature carousel, complete with music for the dolls to ride. Bob's father tells how the promoter of the show came by their booth and looked at the dolls as they were setting up and said, "I hope you have a lot of these dolls, as I have a feeling they won't last long."

Sure enough, even before the show opened, the dealers began to surround the table, buying like crazy. They were fascinated with the dolls' wooden faces, as this was quite revolutionary in the doll-making world. Mr. Robert Raikes Sr. recalls how he was forced to remove some of the dolls from the sales tables or he would have had no merchandise for the collectors when the show opened.

"The response from the public was even more overwhelming," Mr. Raikes Sr. said. "By the first half of the first day of the show, we sold all of the 32 dolls. We grossed $10,000. I couldn't wait to phone my son and tell him the wonderful news."

Bob remembers running through the house after his father phoned shouting, "Bingo! We've hit the right thing at last!"

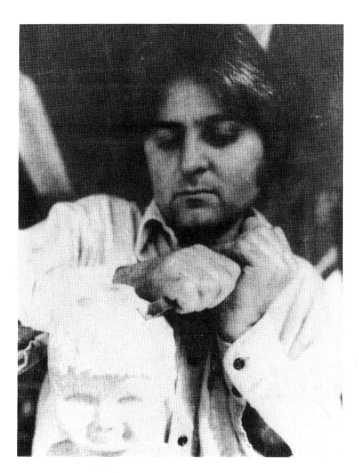

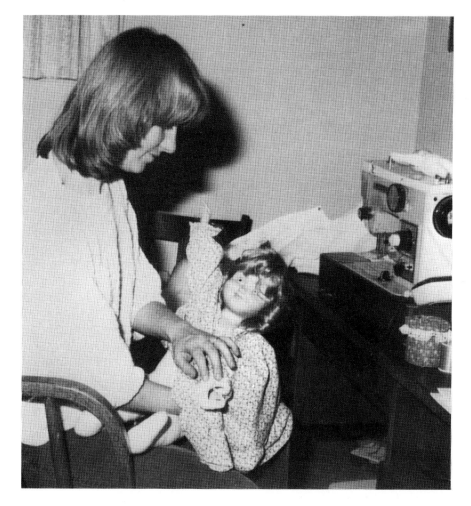

As more and more collectors requested Robert Raikes dolls, he decided to put all his efforts into just making dolls. Courtesy of Mount Shasta Herald.

Robert and Carol Raikes posed for this group portrait with a selection of their hand-carved wooden dolls for the Mount Shasta Herald *in 1982. Courtesy of Mount Shasta Herald.*

Working right along with her husband, Carol Raikes spent hours at her sewing machine creating the bodies and the outfits for the Raikes original dolls. Courtesy of Mount Shasta Herald.

For the next four years, Bob and Carol diligently worked to the early hours of the morning creating dolls. Bob carved. Carol sewed the bodies and the clothes. Bob's parents did their part, too. They agreed to work all the Southern California shows.

Around 1981, Bob began to see teddy bears enter into the doll scene and become quite popular. So, in 1982, he ventured into the teddy bear market. Mr. Raikes Sr. came up with a name for Bob's new creations; they were to be called *Woody Bears*.

When the bears were first introduced, Mr. Raikes Sr. recalls they did not receive quite the favorable response as the dolls. Their faces and feet were carved wood with jointed fur bodies that were stuffed very compactly and as a result, were quite heavy.

"The collector's first response was to touch their wooden faces," said Bob's father.

Cathy Raikes said, "I was surprised by the number of men that were fascinated by the bears and how they were made. They appeared to appreciate them as a form of art."

Each show the sale of bears increased. It was not long before the sales of bears equaled that of the dolls. Because of the increase in demand for their bears, Bob's brother, Mike, the wood shop teacher at Mount Shasta High School, assembled the joints and stuffed the bears, while his wife, Cindy, helped Carol make the bodies.

"I had so much work I didn't know what to do," Bob explained. "It's been a tremendous journey for us." He gives credit to his devoted wife, Carol, by stating, "I can't say enough about the support my wife has given me."

By 1984, Bob and Carol had reached a point in their career when, although they were at last successful and had become recognized artists making a fairly good income, they were literally exhausted from putting in extremely long hours. They reinvested the profits back into the business, but with traveling expenses, rising costs of material and general overhead, the business did not show enough profit to warrant the hours they were working.

When asked one time at a show if he sold wholesale, Bob replied, "It seems like our product has always been retail/wholesale. We would sell for what we thought was retail and people would buy it and resell it." He went on to say, "By being really fair in keeping our prices low, I found this really promoted my product in those early days."

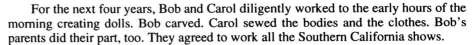

Pouty Boy Doll. Circa 1981. A Robert Raikes original. Approximate size 21 in (53cm) tall; hand-carved wooden head, shoulder plate, hair and hands; cloth body; hand-painted brown eyes and blonde hair; hand-signed and numbered (B-31). Dressed in blue denim trousers and waistcoat with checkered shirt.

Early version of a Raikes pouty boy doll. Courtesy of Cathy and Robert Raikes Sr.

Jennifer Raikes at four years old cuddles one of her father's early creations. Courtesy of Mount Shasta Herald.

(Left) Boy Doll. 1981. A Robert Raikes original. 21in (53cm) tall; hand-carved wooden head, hair, shoulder plate and hands; cloth body; hand-painted brown hair and brown eyes; hand-carved on shoulder plate "Raikes '81 #B5." Dressed in green wool pants, white shirt and knitted brown wool vest. (Right) Girl Doll. 1981. A Robert Raikes original. 21in (53cm) tall; hand-carved wooden head, shoulder plate and hands; cloth body; hand-painted blue eyes; brown synthetic hair; hand-carved on shoulder plate "Raikes #5 '81." Dressed in pink, blue and white check dress; white pinafore.

Not too much detail was given to the carving of the hands of these early dolls. Courtesy of Cathy and Robert Raikes Sr.

A group of hand-carved pieces by Robert Raikes. Courtesy of Robert and Carol Raikes.

Around 1981, Robert Raikes began to see teddy bears enter into the doll scene and become quite popular. So in 1982, he ventured into the teddy bear market. These rare examples of Robert Raikes first designs of teddy bears have hand-carved applied wooden noses and less pronounced features. Also, the eyes on these early designs were not "inset." Approximately ten of this design were produced. (Left) Woody Bear. 1983. A Robert Raikes original. 22in (56cm) tall; gold acrylic fur; hand-carved wooden face and foot pads; applied hand-carved wooden nose; yellow plastic eyes; hand-painted features; jointed arms and legs; swivel head; hand-signed, dated and numbered on foot in black ink "Raikes '83 B.B.101." (Center) Woody Bear. 1983. A Robert Raikes original. 17in (43cm) tall; pale beige acrylic fur; hand-carved wooden face and foot pads; applied hand-carved wooden nose; yellow plastic eyes; hand-painted features; jointed arms and legs; swivel head; hand-signed, dated and numbered on foot in black ink "Raikes '83 M.B.101." (Right) Woody Bear. 1983. A Robert Raikes original. 21in (53cm) tall; gray variegated acrylic fur; hand-carved wooden face and foot pads; applied carved wooden nose; yellow plastic eyes; hand-painted features; jointed arms and legs; swivel head; hand-signed, dated and numbered on foot in black ink "Raikes '83 B.B.100." Courtesy of Cathy and Robert Raikes Sr.

While working on this book with Bob at his home in Tucson, Arizona, I was delighted to have a sneak preview of a magnificent small carousel goat he was working on in his workshop.

The young couple decided to approach various toy companies. They proposed a plan whereby Bob would design the bears and dolls and the companies would manufacture them. When they arranged a meeting with a well-known gift company, Applause (renowned for their products such as Smurfs and Walt Disney characters), the representatives of the company appeared to like the dolls more than the bears. However, they decided to manufacture the bears first as they were easier to reproduce than the dolls.

So, in 1984, a contract was signed and Robert Raikes licensed Applause to produce his creations. (For more information on Applause, please refer to Chapter Five—Robert Raikes' Designs Find a Home With Applause). In addition to the royalties Bob and his wife received for the design of the Robert Raikes "Original Line" for Applause, they still produced special order bears under the name *Woody Bear*.

The Applause bears, designed by Robert Raikes, were an instant success. Applause sold out the first edition of 7500 in three weeks. When the bears reached the retail stores, the situation was similar. Collectors frantically drove all over the country trying to find a store that had at least one Robert Raikes bear for sale.

As the second edition was not scheduled to be released for ten months, there was quite a period before there would be more Robert Raikes bears on the market. So the suspense and interest in his products grew immensely among the collectors. By the time the second edition was released to the stores, its popularity became even more incredible. Collectors had purchased the bears from the catalogs before they even arrived in the stores.

"It was amazing," Bob told me. "There has hardly ever been a time when there are a lot of my products on the market." And so it goes on, edition after edition.

It has been five years to date since the first Robert Raikes bears appeared on the market, but their popularity continues to grow. With each edition, more and more collectors are captured by their warmth and unique appeal.

Unable to meet the increasing demand for his original teddy bears and dolls, Robert Raikes approached the well-known gift company Applause to produce his creations. In 1984, a contract was signed. This is an early grouping of the first edition of Raikes creations (including Jamie *and* Sherwood*) reproduced by Applause in 1985. Note: In the early stages of production of the first edition,* Hucklebear *has* Woody Bear *embroidered on his pocket and* Eric *also has* Woody Bear *knitted into his scarf. The name was soon changed in both cases to* Raikes Bears. *In addition,* Chelsea's *outfit was slightly different at this time. (For more information on these bears, please refer to page 77.) Courtesy of Robert and Carol Raikes.*

Boy Doll. Circa 1976. A Robert Raikes original. 27in (69cm) tall; hand-carved wooden head, shoulder plate and hair; sawdust-filled cloth body; hand-painted blue eyes; hand-signed, dated and numbered on shoulder plate. Dressed in blue denim suit and red and white checked shirt.

Robert Raikes felt his first dolls were rather primitive-looking with long heavy bodies. As not too many of this early representation of Raikes dolls were produced, they are quite sought-after by collectors today. Courtesy of Robert and Carol Raikes.

Chapter Four

Girl Doll. Circa 1975. A Robert Raikes original. Approximately size 28in (71cm) tall; hand-carved wooden head and shoulder plate; sawdust-filled cloth body; hand-painted eyes and eyelashes; black cotton yarn hair; hand-signed, dated and numbered on shoulder plate. Dressed in white and yellow floral print dress with white pinafore and yellow and white gingham hat.

One of the earliest examples of Robert Raikes dolls. Note sculptured cloth hands, hand-painted eyelashes and cotton yarn hair. Courtesy of Robert and Carol Raikes.

How Raikes' Dolls and Bears Came To Be

The creative work of Robert Raikes is visible all over America and also in parts of Europe and the Orient. The response from the public is overwhelming. What is it about his work that has captivated thousands of people of all ages in all walks of life? His creations are unlike almost anything on the market. They have a gentle, unique appeal. The fact that they are carved in wood in a natural style makes people react to them as if they were alive.

For years Robert Raikes was consumed by the desire to be a carver. He found himself caught up with the decisions of creating pieces just for the sheer fun of it or concentrating on turning his avocation into a profitable business that could support his wife and growing young family. Fortunately for the ambitious young carver, he found success in a sphere of his work that he enjoyed and was also profitable—creating dolls and teddy bears.

Although Robert Raikes is renowned for his teddy bears, he first became well-known as an artist in the doll world.

In 1975, when Bob was first commissioned to carve several dolls, he had never been to a doll show or was even aware of the existence of such an event. His first attempts were purely his own concept of how a doll should look. These early designs had a lot of character and people responded to them. However, Bob felt they were rather primitive.

Today, these dolls are highly prized collector's items as only a few of them were ever made.

Characteristic of these first Raikes dolls were hand-carved wooden heads and shoulder plates, painted eyes and sawdust-filled cloth bodies with long arms and legs. The girls' hair was made of long cotton yarn, whereas the boys' hair was sculptured. Due to the weight of the bodies stuffed with sawdust, within a year this was changed to the lighter polyester fiberfilled stuffing. Cloth hands were changed to hand-carved wood. The wood on the lower part of the arm varied in length. In addition, attractive synthetic wigs replaced the girls' cotton yarn hair.

The first three to four years of doll making Bob spent developing several different size little girl dolls, along with a few boy dolls. His goal at this point was to develop his skills in this field and create his own design of artist dolls. From the beginning,

(Left) Girl Doll. 1978. A Robert Raikes original. 27in (69cm) tall; hand-carved wooden head and shoulder plate; sawdust-filled cloth body; hand-painted brown eyes; brown synthetic hair (replaced); carved on shoulder plate "#1 Raikes '78." Dressed in red and white dress.

Early version of Raikes' dolls. Long heavy cloth body. The doll originally came with cotton yarn hair.

(Right) Jason. Pouty-face Boy Doll. 1975. A Robert Raikes original. 27in (69cm) tall; hand-carved head, shoulder plate and hair; sawdust-filled cloth body; hand-painted brown eyes, blonde hair; hand-carved on shoulder plate "Jason #1 '75." Dressed in black velvet suit and white shirt.

Named after Bob's son, Jason. Experimenting with facial expressions, Raikes created a line of pouty-face dolls. The inspiration came for this expressive childlike little face from observing his young son, Jason. Courtesy of Robert and Carol Raikes.

(Left) Girl Doll. 1977. A Robert Raikes original. 14in (36cm) tall; hand-carved wooden head and shoulder plate; cloth body; hand-painted blue eyes; brown synthetic hair; hand-carved on shoulder plate "RWR '77." Dressed in blue, pink and white floral dress with matching hat.

(Right) Girl Doll. 1978. A Robert Raikes original. 15in (38cm) tall; hand-carved wooden head and shoulder plate; cloth body; hand-painted brown eyes; brown synthetic hair; hand-carved on shoulder plate "Raikes '78." Dressed in dark blue floral print dress.

Examples of Robert Raikes' early dolls. Note primitive carved features compared to his later work. Courtesy of Robert and Cathy Raikes Sr.

Pouty-face Boy Doll. 1980. A Robert Raikes original. 22in (56cm) tall; hand-carved wooden head, hair, shoulder plate and hands; cloth body; hand-painted blonde hair and blue eyes; hand-carved on shoulder plate "B2 Raikes 1980." Dressed in Levi overalls and red knitted sweater.

Wonderful hand-carved pouty-face. Note early primitive carved hands with no separation between fingers, sculptured tears on cheek. Courtesy of Nancy Page.

Gnome. 1980. A Robert Raikes original. 9in (23cm) tall; all hand-carved wood; hand-painted features; articulated head and body; separate hand-carved pipe and cane; clothes made of wool and dyed burlap. Hand-carved on back "Raikes."

One of the earliest dressed characters created by Robert Raikes. Courtesy of Robert and Carol Raikes.

Girl Doll. Circa 1981. A Robert Raikes original. Approximate size 17in (43cm) tall; hand-carved wooden head; shoulder plate; hands, lower legs and shoes; cloth body; hand-painted brown eyes; black synthetic hair; hand-signed, dated and numbered (SG27). Dressed in white and dark blue printed dress with white apron.

Early version of Raikes small cloth-bodied girl dolls. Note carved wooden shoes. Courtesy of Robert and Cathy Raikes Sr.

A hang-tag "Hand Carved and Crafted Dolls by Bob and Carol Raikes" was attached to each doll. The tags for the dolls varied somewhat over the years. Courtesy of Robert and Cathy Raikes Sr.

Hand Carved
and
Crafted Dolls

CUSTOM MADE DOLLS AVAILABLE

BOB AND CAROL RAIKES   772-7189

Boy Doll. Circa 1981. A Robert Raikes original. Approximate size 17in (43cm) tall; hand-carved wooden head, shoulder plate, hair, hands, lower legs and shoes; cloth body; hand-painted hair and eyes; hand-signed, dated and numbered. Dressed in black suit, white shirt and checkered hat.

The smaller size in the Raikes cloth bodied dolls were very slender with daintily carved features. Not much detail was given to the carving of the hands and shoes of these early dolls. Courtesy of Robert and Cathy Raikes Sr.

Raikes Originals
PRESENTS
Jensine
Handcarved
From the hands and imagination of
Robert Raikes
Mt. Shasta, CA 96067
No._____
Date_____
Robert W. Raikes

A "Raikes Originals" certificate of authenticity for the dolls. This certificate accompanied each doll produced by Robert Raikes. The name and number of that particular doll, the date it was made was hand-written on each certificate. The design of the certificate changed over the years but the information remained the same. Courtesy of Robert and Carol Raikes.

Jenny. Girl Doll. 1981. A Robert Raikes original. 25in (64cm) tall; hand-carved wooden head, shoulder plate and hands; cloth body; "big" blue painted eyes; light brown synthetic hair; hand-carved on shoulder plate "Raikes '81 #G6." Dressed in blue print dress with a white pinafore.

Robert Raikes named this doll after his eldest daughter, Jenny. One of the "big-eyed" series of dolls. Courtesy of Robert and Pat Woodman. Photograph by Robert Woodman.

Three examples of Robert Raikes' original basic doll designs showing the progression of his work.

(Right) First design. Girl Doll. 1978. Hand-carved wooden head and shoulder plate; hand-painted features; cloth body; long arms and legs; heavy sawdust-filled body; replaced synthetic wig (original wig was made of cotton yarn.

(Center) Second design. Boy Doll. 1981. Hand-carved wooden head, hair, shoulder plate and hands; cloth polyester-filled body; hand-painted features.

Note the changes from the first design. The hands are now hand-carved wood. The body is changed to the lighter polyester stuffing. The limbs are in more proportion to the body and not so long. The head is affixed to the body in a neater, more professional manner. The bodies on the girl dolls were also changed to this design. In addition, the girls' hair was changed from cotton yarn to synthetic hair.

(Left) Third design. Girl Doll. 1985. All hand-carved wood, articulated head and body; hand-painted features; synthetic hair.

In 1982, Robert Raikes began experimenting with carved wooden bodies with what he called "sophisticated joints." By 1987, the bodies of all Raikes dolls were completely carved of wood and jointed. Cloth-bodied dolls were only made by special order. Courtesy of Robert and Cathy Raikes Sr.

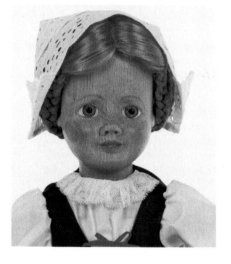

Girl Doll. Circa 1981. A Robert Raikes original. 24in (61cm) tall; hand-carved wooden head, shoulder plate and hands; cloth body; hand-painted blue eyes; hand-signed, dated and numbered. Dressed in an Austrian-style outfit.

Note how artistic-looking Raikes' dolls have become since his first attempt in 1975. Courtesy of Robert and Carol Raikes.

Clown Doll. 1982. A Robert Raikes original. 22in (56cm) tall; hand-carved wooden head, shoulder plate and hands; cloth body; hand-painted eyes and clown face; yellow cotton yarn hair; hand-carved on shoulder plate "Raikes '82 #20." Dressed in red check with white collar clown suit.

Clown is seated on a metal tricycle made by Robert Raikes Sr. Courtesy of Cathy and Robert Raikes Sr.

Girl Doll. Circa 1981. A Robert Raikes original. 24in (61cm) tall; hand-carved wooden head, shoulder plate and hands; cloth body; brown synthetic hair; hand-painted "big" brown eyes; hand-signed, dated and numbered. Dressed in a pink and blue dress.

Exploring the limits of expression, Robert Raikes produced a small series of dolls with big painted eyes. They are referred to as the Raikes "big-eyed" series. Note that more detail is now given to the hands. Courtesy of Robert and Carol Raikes.

Jester *Doll. Circa 1982. A Robert Raikes original. 18in (46cm) tall; hand-carved wooden head shoulder plate and hands; cloth body; hand-painted eyes and face; red cotton yarn hair; hand-signed, dated and numbered. Dressed in a white, red and blue satin clown outfit.* Courtesy of Robert and Carol Raikes.

Clown *Doll. 1982. A Robert Raikes original. 24in (61cm) tall; hand-carved wooden head, shoulder plate and hands; cloth body; hand-painted eyes and face; orange synthetic curly hair; hand-carved on shoulder plate "Raikes '82 #14B." Dressed in multi-colored striped clown outfit.*

The clown holds hand-carved wooden juggling balls. The large shoes were made by Robert Raikes' father. Courtesy of Robert and Pat Woodman. Photograph by Robert Woodman.

Clown *Doll. Circa 1982. A Robert Raikes original. 22in (56cm) tall; hand-carved wooden head, shoulder plate and hands; cloth body; hand-painted blue eyes and clown face; sections of gathered red material for hair; hand-carved on shoulder plate "Raikes G327." Dressed in bright orange and red floral clown suit.* Courtesy of Debby Gong. Photograph by Roy H. Floyd.

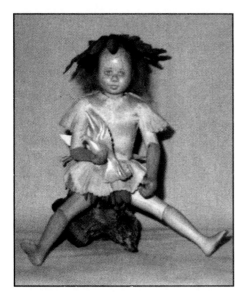

Faerie *Doll. 1983. A Robert Raikes original. Approximate size 9in (23cm) tall; all hand-carved wood; articulated head and body; hand-painted blue eyes; synthetic brown hair; hand-signed and dated.*

First all hand-carved wooden Faerie *doll Robert Raikes created. Courtesy of Robert and Carol Raikes.*

Bob was interested in making each doll look different, with its own character. He sincerely felt that each collector deserved something that was truly unique.

Experimenting with facial expressions early in his doll-making career, Bob began creating a line of pouty-face dolls. The inspiration came for this expressive childlike little face from observing his young son, Jason.

After attending doll shows, Bob was fascinated by the soft beauty of the faces of the bisque antique dolls. Exhibiting at shows also put Bob in close contact with the collectors. Inspired by the antique dolls and conversing with the collectors, the enthusiastic young sculptor went on to create his series of "Little Wooden Children."

Each new doll produced was more sophisticated and intriguing than the last. The utmost detail was applied to the features. The bodies became much lighter and shapelier. A metal armature encased within the stuffing of the arms of the cloth-bodied dolls was designed to enable the arms to be posed or to hold a toy. Approximately 600 Raikes dolls were made with cloth bodies, the majority being sizes 24in (61cm), 14in (36cm) and a few smaller.

In 1982, Bob began experimenting with carved wooden bodies, with what he called "sophisticated joints." With his past experience in carving all-wood human sculptures, Bob found this type of body a natural and easy transition. However, the hard part was to accomplish the jointing method.

By 1987, the bodies of all Raikes dolls were completely carved of wood and jointed. Cloth bodies were only made by special order.

Now these graceful elegant dolls could be posed.

Bob prided himself that no two dolls were alike. The many different expressions and varieties of dolls this talented artist created brought accolades from all corners.

Bob hand-carved or hand-signed in ink his signature on the back of the all-wooden dolls and on the back of the shoulder plate of the dolls with cloth bodies. They were also dated and came with a certificate of authenticity.

(Left) Peter. *Boy Doll. 1982. A Robert Raikes original. 23in (58cm) tall; hand-carved wooden head, shoulder plate, hair and hands; cloth body; hand-painted blue eyes and blonde hair; hand-carved on shoulder plate "Raikes '82 B28." Dressed in black velvet pants, variegated brown knitted vest, white shirt and brown and white wool hat.*
(Right) Shanna. *Girl Doll. 1982. A Robert Raikes original. 22in (56cm) tall; hand-carved face, shoulder plate and hands; cloth body; hand-painted brown eyes; blonde synthetic hair; hand-carved on shoulder plate "Raikes '82 G114." Dressed in gray and white print dress; white pinafore.*

A metal armature is encased within the stuffing of the arms of both dolls to allow the arms to be posed or hold a toy. Courtesy of Peter and Janice Spitzer.

Jensine. *Black Girl Doll. 1983. A Robert Raikes original. 23in (58cm) tall; hand-carved wooden head, shoulder plate and hands; cloth body; hand-painted brown eyes; black synthetic hair; hand-carved on shoulder plate "Raikes '83 G275." Dressed in pink print dress with white cotton pinafore.*

Robert Raikes made very few versions of a black doll. Courtesy of Peter and Janice Spitzer.

A selection of Robert Raikes original hand-carved wooden doll heads, waiting to be assembled onto the cloth bodies. Note the wonderful variety of facial expressions. In some cases, before Bob made the bodies for the dolls, he would carve several different doll heads with different expressions and mail them to the collectors to choose the face they preferred. Courtesy of Robert and Carol Raikes.

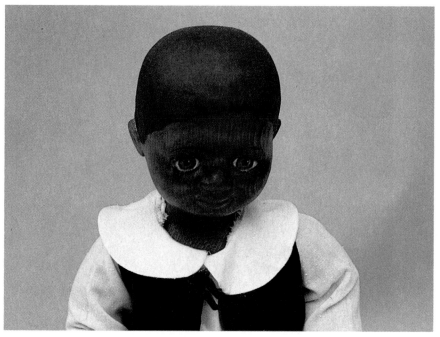

Black Boy Doll. 1983. A Robert Raikes original. 22in (56cm) tall; hand-carved wooden head, hair, shoulder plate and hands; cloth body, hand-painted black hair, brown eyes; hand-carved on shoulder plate "B89 Raikes '83." Dressed in black velvet suit and white shirt.

Robert Raikes produced a very limited number of black boy dolls. Courtesy of Cathy and Robert Raikes Sr.

Jester Doll. 1984. A Robert Raikes original. Approximately 18in (46cm) tall; all hand-carved wood; articulated head and body; hand-painted eyes and face; brown feathers for hair; hand-signed and dated. Dressed in dark purple satin costume. Courtesy of Robert and Carol Raikes.

Witch Doll. 1983. A Robert Raikes original. 16in (41cm) tall; hand-carved wooden head; shoulder plate and hands; cloth body; black synthetic hair; hand-painted eyes; hand-signed and dated. Dressed in a black dress and cape.
One-of-a-kind. Note the intricately carved features. Robert Raikes created the Witch *to exhibit at a doll show. She originally held a carved wooden apple with a worm crawling out of it.* Courtesy of Robert and Carol Raikes.

Medieval Jester. 1984. A Robert Raikes original. 23in (58cm) tall; all hand-carved wood; articulated head and body; hand-painted eyes and face; black synthetic hair; hand-signed and dated. Dressed as a jester.
Magnificent example of the exquisite workmanship of Robert Raikes' later work. Note unusual wrist joints. Courtesy of Robert and Carol Raikes.

Girl Doll. 1984. A Robert Raikes original. Approximately 26in (66cm) tall; all hand-carved wood; articulated head and body; hand-painted brown eyes; brown synthetic hair; hand-signed and dated. Dressed in blue and white dress.

As each individual all hand-carved wood doll was so unique and not part of an edition, they were not numbered, only hand signed and dated. Courtesy of Robert and Carol Raikes.

Gretal. *Girl Doll. 1984. A Robert Raikes original. Approximately 26in (66cm) tall; all hand-carved wood; articulated head and body; hand-painted blue eyes; blonde synthetic hair; hand-signed and dated. Dressed in a German-style costume.*

Note how the hands and features have even more detail with each doll Raikes creates. Courtesy of Robert and Carol Raikes.

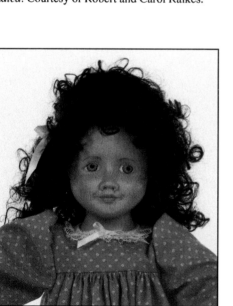

Girl Doll. 1984. A Robert Raikes original. Approximately 26in (66cm) tall; all hand-carved wood; articulated head and body; hand-painted blue eyes; black synthetic hair; hand-signed and dated. Dressed in a long rose pink and white print dress. Courtesy of Robert and Carol Raikes.

Gretal. *Girl Doll. 1984. A Robert Raikes original. 26in (66cm) tall; all hand-carved wood; articulated head and body. Undressed version showing the workmanship of Raikes all hand-carved wood doll body.* Courtesy of Robert and Carol Raikes.

Faerie *Doll. 1984. A Robert Raikes original. Approximately 12in (31cm) tall; all hand-carved wood; articulated head and body; hand-painted eyes; synthetic brown hair; hand-signed and dated. Dressed in dark green tulle skirt with silk flowers and feather accessories.*

Raikes, always into his imagination, gives life to Faeries. *Produced between 1983 to 1986, the majority stand about 12in (31cm) tall. Approximately eight were made, as their very delicate features were extremely difficult to produce.* Courtesy of Robert and Carol Raikes.

Faerie *Doll. 1984. A Robert Raikes original. 12in (31cm) tall; all hand-carved wood; articulated head and body; hand-painted blue eyes; synthetic brown hair; hand-signed and dated. Dressed in dark lavender silk skirt and top in the shape of flower petals.*

Approximately eight Raikes Faerie dolls were produced between 1983 and 1986. Courtesy of Robert and Carol Raikes.

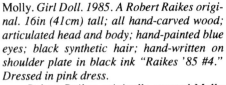

Molly. *Girl Doll. 1985. A Robert Raikes original. 16in (41cm) tall; all hand-carved wood; articulated head and body; hand-painted blue eyes; black synthetic hair; hand-written on shoulder plate in black ink "Raikes '85 #4." Dressed in pink dress.*

Robert Raikes originally created Molly *as a Christmas present for his mother. It was one of Bob's favorite dolls. He later made approximately three versions of this cute little girl doll. Reproduced by The Good Company in 1989.* Courtesy of Robert and Carol Raikes.

Baby Doll. 1985. A Robert Raikes original. 21in (53cm) tall; hand-carved wooden head, hair, shoulder plate and hands; cloth body; hand-painted blonde hair and blue eyes; hand-signed. Dressed in an early christening dress and bonnet.

One-of-a-kind. Created for Robert Raikes' mother. Reproduced by The Good Company in 1989. Courtesy of Cathy and Robert Raikes Sr.

Little Red Riding Hood. *1984. A Robert Raikes original. 25in (64cm) tall; all hand-carved wood; articulated head and body; hand-painted eyes; brown synthetic hair; hand-signed and dated. Dressed in blue and white check skirt, blue and white print blouse and red cape.* Courtesy of Peter and Janice Spitzer.

Because the all-wood dolls were so unique from each other and not part of editions, these dolls were not numbered. From the 800 dolls the imaginative artist produced, approximately 250 were not numbered. Also, as the dolls became more sophisticated, Bob decided to change the name of the "Little Wooden Children" to "Raikes Originals" (approximately 1982).

The dolls at that time were the family's entire source of income. The business was on the level of a cottage industry, being conducted out of the Raikes' home. Everyone became involved in their construction and sale.

The Raikes' home and workshop were filled with dolls in various stages of production. The children were continually surrounded by dolls to cuddle and play with. Bob describes what his house was like in those early doll-making days.

"A doll-making studio was a hectic environment in which to raise a family," Bob recalls. "There was a carving shop, a material storage room and an assembly sewing room. This sometimes overflowed into the living room, even though we tried to avoid it in order to keep an orderly house for the family. This was not always easy to do."

It took Bob and Carol approximately two days to make the small dolls and two or three weeks for some of the larger or more complicated ones. They worked 12 to 16 hours days.

Carol Raikes took care of the bookkeeping and also made numerous different outfits for all the dolls. It was also Carol's job to find a name that suited each doll. Carol said, "I looked through books and encyclopedias for hours looking for that perfect name."

It was the Raikes' children, Jason, Jenny and Emily's responsibility to give the dolls their final inspection before they were packed to go to the show.

By exhibiting their son's work at numerous doll shows, Bob's parents, Robert Raikes Sr. and his wife, Cathy, played an active and very supportive part in their son's career. Robert Raikes Sr. kept a record of every person that purchased Bob's early dolls from him. He would tell the collectors, "Someday my son will be really famous, and he may wish to contact you regarding events that may interest you about his work." Sure enough, Bob's father's words came true and his conscientious work paid off. Approximately the first 1000 people that were contacted regarding the Robert Raikes Collector's Club, formed in June 1988, were names the proud father had so faithfully saved for all these years.

Looking back at those shows, Bob's father describes what Bob's dolls remind him of. "When the dolls were displayed at the shows, they reminded me of a group of school children as each one was so different."

Raikes has an uncanny ability to bring fantasy to a tangible state. For instance, his children and animal dolls are the sort that demand to be picked up and played with. Although they are fully jointed, poseable and wear beautifully made removeable outfits, it is their facial expressions which beckon the viewer. The animal dolls each have distinct personalities and seem like characters from childhood bedtime stories. Carol Raikes dressed these fantasy creatures with perfection and skill.

Raikes, always into his imagination, also gives life to fairies. Produced between 1983 and 1986, they stand approximately 1ft (31cm) tall and are all that your dreams could conjure up. Approximately eight were made, as their very delicate features were extremely hard to produce.

As the dolls were individually hand-carved, Bob never knew as he was carving what their final expression would really be until the work was completed. He let the doll take on its own character. He knew what the basic look would be (e.g., smiling or pouty). "The face has to evoke emotion or a sense of wonder from those viewing the dolls on my end. I have to feel the work has challenged my creativity. In some cases, before I made the body for the doll, I would carve several doll heads with different expressions and mail them to the collectors to choose the face they preferred," Bob explained.

Little Red Riding Hood. *1983. A Robert Raikes original. 26in (66cm) tall; all hand-carved wood; articulated head and body; hand-painted brown eyes; blonde synthetic hair. Dressed in a blue and white dress with red cape.*
Wolf *Doll. 1983. A Robert Raikes original. 30in (76cm) tall; hand-carved wood head, shoulder plate, legs and paws; cloth body; hand-painted features; hand-signed in gold ink on* shoulder plate "Robert Raikes 1983." Dressed in a gray check wool suit with white and gray striped shirt and red scarf.

Wolf *sits on original hand-carved wooden tree stump. Hand-signed in gold ink on stump "Robert Raikes 1983." Note the fine detail in the carved mouth and tongue. Robert Raikes created two different versions of* Little Red Riding Hood and the Wolf. *Courtesy of Debby Gong.*

Skier. *Boy Doll. 1985. A Robert Raikes origi-nal. Approximately 21in (53cm) tall; hand-carved wooden head, shoulder plate, hair and hands; cloth body; hand-painted blonde hair and brown eyes; hand-signed, dated and num-bered. Dressed as boy skier in black pants, white shirt and knitted red scarf and ski cap. He holds a hand-carved wooden pair of skis and ski poles.*

Robert Raikes only designed "one" skier. Courtesy of Robert and Carol Raikes.

Girl Doll. 1985. A Robert Raikes original. 17in (43cm) tall; hand-carved wooden head, shoul-der plate, hands, lower legs and shoes; cloth body; hand-painted blue eyes; brown synthetic hair; hand-written in brown ink on shoulder plate "H52 Raikes '85." Dressed in white floral dress with pink and white polka dotted pin-afore.

Note carved wooden shoes. Courtesy of Robert and Pat Woodman. Photograph by Rob-ert Woodman.

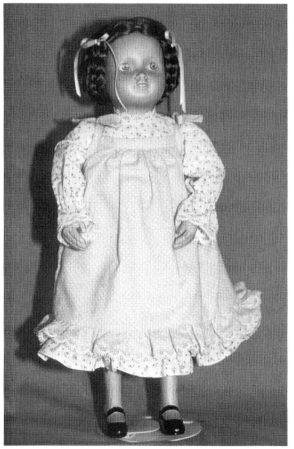

Fawn *Doll. 1986. A Robert Raikes original. 20in (50cm) tall; all hand-carved wood; ar-ticulated head and body; hand-painted brown eyes; synthetic light brown hair; hand-signed and dated.*

One-of-a-kind. Note jointed wrists, carved hooves and teeth. Courtesy of Robert and Carol Raikes.

(Left) Janice. *Girl Doll. 1985. A Robert Raikes original. 26in (66cm) tall; all hand-carved wood; articulated head and body; hand-painted brown eyes; synthetic blonde hair; hand-written in brown ink "Robert Raikes 1985." Dressed in pink and white stripe dress, blue apron and scarf.*

Note smiling face and carved teeth.
(Center) Jordan. *Girl Doll. 1984. A Robert Raikes original. 23in (58cm) tall; hand-carved wooden head, shoulder plate and hands; cloth body; hand-painted brown eyes; synthetic brown hair; hand-written on shoulder plate in brown ink "Raikes G84 '82." Dressed in cream and blue-colored polka dot dress trimmed with lace.*
(Right) Cheryl. *Girl Doll. 1982. A Robert Raikes original. 23.5in (58cm) tall; hand-carved wooden head, shoulder plate and hands; cloth body; hand-painted blue eyes; blonde synthetic hair; hand-written on shoulder plate in brown ink "G102 Raikes '82." Dressed in gray and white print dress with lace trim.*

Jordan *and* Cheryl *both have wire armature encased within the stuffing of the arms to allow the arms to be posed or hold a toy.* Courtesy of Peter and Janice Spitzer.

Pioneer Lady *Doll. 1985. A Robert Raikes original. Approximately 18in (46cm) tall; all hand-carved wood; articulated head and body; hand-painted brown eyes; brown synthetic hair; hand-painted brown eyes; brown synthetic hair; hand-signed. Dressed in blue and black dress with matching hat and white apron.*

Robert Raikes produced four versions of the Pioneer Lady *in different outfits.* Courtesy of Robert and Carol Raikes.

Boy *Doll. 1985. A Robert Raikes original. Approximate size 21in (53cm) tall; hand-carved wooden head, shoulder plate, hair and hands; cloth body; hand-painted hair and eyes; hand-signed, dated and numbered. Dressed in short wool trousers and cap, white shirt and knitted vest.*

Robert Raikes' boy dolls are considered highly collectible as only a small percentage of the dolls he produced were boys. Courtesy of Robert and Carol Raikes.

Winter Lady *Doll. 1986. A Robert Raikes original. Approximately 18in (46cm) tall; all hand-carved wood; articulated head and body; hand-painted eyes; black synthetic hair; hand-signed and dated. Dressed in brown silk skirt, cape and hat and white blouse, carrying fur muff. Courtesy of Robert and Carol Raikes.*

Oriental Lady *Doll. 1986. A Robert Raikes original. 22in (56cm) tall; all hand-carved wood including hair; articulated head and body; hand-painted brown eyes; black hair; hand-written on back "Raikes 1986." Dressed in maroon and white silk kimono (six layers of silk in kimono).*

Only two Raikes' Oriental Ladies were made. One doll had synthetic hair and one had hand-carved, black painted hair. Courtesy of Peter and Janice Spitzer.

Faerie *Doll. 1986. A Robert Raikes original. 12in (31cm) tall; all hand-carved wood; articulated head and body; hand-painted brown eyes; synthetic brown hair; hand-signed and dated. Dressed in green tulle skirt with silk flowers.*

Note very delicate carved features. Courtesy of Robert and Carol Raikes.

When I asked the enterprising artist if he would name the various dolls he made, the year and the amount produced, he replied, "Linda, too much time has passed, and I have designed too many different items to be able to remember exact dates and numbers. I was always so busy trying to keep up with all the orders. At the time, I never realized the importance of keeping such records."

However, he talked enthusiastically of the dolls he could recall. "My favorite dolls are those dealing with fantasy and elegant ladies. It gives me a chance to daydream in art form. The elegant ladies were all-wood except for three. There were approximately 25 produced. Each was different. Several were exquisitely dressed in beautiful silk clothes. I made two Oriental ladies between 1985 and 1986. Each of these had six layers of silk in their beautiful kimonos.

"I only made about three gnomes. The first (1976) was all carved in wood playing a pan flute. He was only 8in (20cm) tall. The next (1979) carried a cane and a pipe. The last gnome I made was in 1983.

"I originally designed the doll Molly as a Christmas present for my mother. It was also one of my favorite dolls. Created in 1985, I later made about three different versions of this cute little girl doll. My mother also persuaded me to make her a baby doll. Molly and Baby were the designs used for the first series of Raikes dolls manufactured by Applause.

Woody Bear. *1982. A Robert Raikes original. 7in (18cm) tall; beige acrylic fur; hand-carved wooden face; applied hand-carved nose; hand-painted features; unjointed body.*
This is the "first" teddy bear Robert Raikes ever made. It was a Christmas present for his mother. Note the small carved features and painted eyes. The nose was hand-carved separately and glued to the snout. Courtesy of Cathy and Robert Raikes Sr.

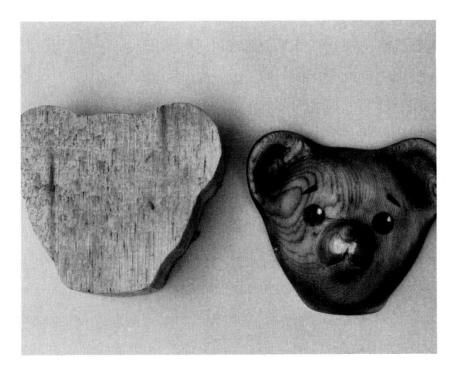

The "first" attempt Robert Raikes made to create a bear's face was in 1982. Note how he originally tried wooden ears, an applied tiny carved nose and hand-painted eyes. This rare and interesting example of Raikes first bear's head would not have been saved had it not been for Robert Raikes Sr., who retrieved it from the trash where his son had discarded it the day before. At this writing, this design has never been reproduced. Courtesy of Cathy and Robert Raikes Sr.

An example of the identification marks on the first designs of Robert Raikes' Woody Bears. Hand-written in black ink, the letters indicate the size of the bear, for example, T.B. (Tiny Bear), S.B. (Small Bear), M.B. (Medium Bear), B.B. (Big Bear). This early identification method was soon changed with the introduction of the entire face of the bear carved from one piece of wood. It appears on these first designs, the numbers (example, #101) did not specify the amount produced. Courtesy of Cathy and Robert Raikes Sr.

Woody Bear (Prototype). 1982. A Robert Raikes original. 22in (56cm) tall; variegated beige acrylic fur; hand-carved wooden face; applied hand-carved wooden nose; hand-painted features; jointed arms and legs; swivel head.

This is an example of one of the earliest designs of Raikes' teddy bears. It was an experimental piece, not made for resale. Note the applied separate hand-carved nose, painted eyes and acrylic fur paw and foot pads. Courtesy of Robert and Carol Raikes.

(Left) Woody Bear. 1983. A Robert Raikes original. 17in (43cm) tall; pale beige acrylic fur; hand-carved wooden face and foot pads; applied hand-carved wooden nose; yellow plastic eyes; jointed arms and legs; swivel head; hand-signed and numbered on foot in black ink. "Raikes 83 MB101." (Right) Woody Bear. 1983. A Robert Raikes original. 22in (56cm) tall; gold acrylic fur; hand-carved wooden face and foot pads; applied hand-carved wooden nose; yellow plastic eyes; jointed arms and legs; swivel head; hand-signed and numbered on foot in black ink "Raikes '83. B.B. 101."

Examples of the first bears Robert Raikes produced for resale. Note the flat face, shorter snout and small applied hand-carved wooden nose. In addition, the eyes on these early bears were not "inset." Also note the hang-tags are the same as used for the dolls. The Woody Bear tags were not yet in use. Approximately ten of this design were made. Raikes then created a more professional and appealing-looking bear with a longer pronounced snout and the face and nose which were all carved from one piece of wood, and the eyes were "inset." Courtesy of Cathy and Robert Raikes Sr.

Woody Bears. *1983. Robert Raikes originals. 7in (18cm) tall; acrylic fur; hand-carved wooden snout; applied carved wooden nose; plastic eyes; unjointed body.*

Examples of one of the experimental designs when Raikes first ventured into the teddy bear world. Approximately four were made. They were never produced for resale. Courtesy of Cathy and Robert Raikes Sr.

Baby Woody Bear. *1983. A Robert Raikes original. 9in (23cm) tall; short beige acrylic fur; hand-carved wooden snout; brown Ultrasuede foot and paw pads; plastic eyes; red felt tongue; jointed arms and legs; swivel head; cry box encased in stomach.*

Approximately two of this design of Raikes' baby bears were produced when Bob was first experimenting with different styles of hand-carved wooden faces. Courtesy of Cathy and Robert Raikes Sr.

Woody Bear *(Prototype). 1983. A Robert Raikes original. 22in (56cm) tall; beige acrylic fur; hand-carved wooden face and foot pads; brown plastic eyes; jointed arms and legs; swivel head.*

Here we see basically the same early design as the bears in the 1983 Woody Bear, but now the artist improves his technique for the nose by skillfully carving the face, snout and nose from one piece of wood. Note the eyes are changed to brown but are still not "inset." Note also the dark shading of the wood which was obtained by burning the wood, an early procedure that was later replaced by allowing the natural grain of the wood to show through. This experimental bear demonstrates the transition between the bear with the applied hand-carved nose to the more professional-looking bear with the face, snout and nose carved from one piece of wood.

Woody Bear. *1983. A Robert Raikes original. 21in (53cm) tall; pale beige acrylic fur; hand-carved wooden face and foot pads (early burnt wood method used); "inset" plastic eyes; jointed arms and legs; swivel head; "hand-stuffed body;" hand-carved on foot "Raikes '83 L025."*

An example of one of the earliest designs of bears produced for resale with the face, snout and nose hand-carved from one piece of wood. Note the characteristic of Robert Raikes' Woody Bears quickly progressed from the crude applied wooden nose to this far more professional-looking bear with the face, nose and snout all hand-carved from one piece of wood. In addition, the eyes are now skillfully inset into the wood. Note also the introduction of the firmer, more sculptured body, also the signature and identification marks are now hand-carved into the wooden foot pads. The tie was an addition to some of the early designs. Courtesy of Peter and Janice Spitzer.

Robert Raikes original bears were hand-carved, signed, dated and numbered on the foot. Most of the bears were signed "Robert Raikes," "R.W. Raikes" or "Raikes." Bob almost always hand-carved the identification marks and his signature, but in some instances he used a permanent ink pen. Note this example is the later form of numbering system. Courtesy of Robert and Pat Woodman. Photograph by Robert Woodman.

Woody Bear. *1983. A Robert Raikes original. 24in (61cm) tall; long variegated beige acrylic fur; hand-carved wooden face and foot pads; inset plastic eyes; jointed arms and legs; swivel head; hard-stuffed body; signed, dated and numbered on foot.*

A wonderful example of an early bear with the burned wood effect. To obtain the look Bob wanted, he burned the wood with a blowtorch. He later accomplished this realistic effect by allowing the natural grain of the wood to show through. This bear was adopted by a collector at Linda Mullins' first San Diego Teddy Bear and Antique Toy Show and Sale in 1983. Courtesy of Robert and Carol Raikes.

Jamie *(Prototype)*. Woody Bear. *1984. A Robert Raikes original. 10in (23cm) tall; short gray acrylic fur; hand-carved wooden face and foot pads; inset plastic eyes; jointed arms and legs; swivel head; hand-carved on foot "Raikes T001 '84."*

Note the earlier method of identification was used on this prototype. The popular design of Jamie *was reproduced by Applause in 1985.* Courtesy of Cathy and Robert Raikes Sr.

Sherwood *(Prototype)*. Woody Bear. *1983. A Robert Raikes original. 14in (36cm) tall; short dark brown acrylic fur; hand-carved wooden face and foot pads; hand-painted freckles; inset plastic eyes; jointed arms and legs; swivel head; hand-carved on foot "Raikes '83 SS014;" label on leg "Raikes Original Woody Bear."*

Raikes' popular design of Sherwood *was reproduced by Applause in 1985.* Courtesy of Cathy and Robert Raikes Sr.

Woody Bear. *1984. A Robert Raikes original. 21in (53cm) tall; long silky smokey blue acrylic fur; hand-carved wooden face and foot pads; inset plastic eyes; jointed arms and legs; swivel head; hard-stuffed body; hand-carved on foot "84 Raikes L21;" hand-signed in gold ink "Robert Raikes."*

One-of-a-kind. Collector gave Bob the beautiful material to make this bear. In the majority of the early bears, hand-carved "wooden pads" were only used on the feet. Courtesy of Peter and Janice Spitzer.

Roller Skater. Woody Bear. *1984. A Robert Raikes original. 15in (38cm) tall; black acrylic fur; hand-carved wooden face and foot pads; inset plastic eyes; jointed arms and legs; swivel head; hard-stuffed body; hand-carved wooden roller skates; hand-carved on foot "Raikes '84 M144."*

Approximately ten in the edition. Courtesy of Cathy and Robert Raikes Sr.

Pirate. Woody Bear. *1984. A Robert Raikes original. 16in (40cm) tall; black with gray fleck acrylic fur; hand-carved wooden face, feet and paw pads; inset plastic eyes; hard-stuffed body; jointed arms and legs; swivel head; hand-carved on foot "Raikes '84 M153;" hand-written in gold ink "Raikes;" cloth tag on leg "Raikes Original Woody Bear." Hand-carved wooden sword; metal hook screwed into paw; black patch over eye; black and tan cotton turban.*

Approximately ten Raikes' Pirates were made between 1984 and 1986. Note how soon Robert Raikes began creating variations to his original Woody Bear *design. Courtesy of Peter and Janice Spitzer.*

"I created two different creations of Little Red Riding Hood with a wolf. Each Red Riding Hood came with a very realistic-looking hand-carved wooden wolf doll. One version of wolf was all-wood and the other had a cloth body.

"I made five different styles of Goldilocks. The bears were sold separately.

"In 1983, I designed a very scary-looking witch to exhibit at a doll show. She had lots of character with intricately carved features. Her body was cloth, with carved wooden hands and feet. Dressed in black, she carried a bundle of sticks and held a carved wooden apple with a worm crawling out of it.

"I produced about 25 clowns from 1977 to 1986. All were different. The majority had cloth bodies and were 24in (61cm) tall. In 1984, I made a Medieval Jester doll. It was all-wood, with articulated head and body. Even the wrists were jointed. It was a fun doll to design and make.

"The big-eyed (large painted eyes) series of dolls were made from 1981 to 1982. Approximately 12 were produced. I was exploring the limits of expression.

"I also remember making three Prairie Women, two Indians, one boy skier and a queen doll. I am sure there are many other designs I haven't mentioned, as collectors would give me unusual requests, and I like nothing more than the challenge of creating something new."

The vigorous and dedicated young sculptor crams as much as he can into life. He looks at each new piece he carves as a learning process that takes him into the next level. This is how he comes up with so many ideas; he never dwells on one piece. He can hardly wait to complete a design as he is always anxious to move on to the next idea.

The road from "birds to bears" was not an easy one for the persevering young sculptor. But in 1982, when Bob decided to venture into the growing world of teddy bears, he found he had discovered a true winner. His was a brand new kind of teddy bear. Immediately recognizable by their appealing hand-carved wooden faces, they were marketed under the name of *Woody Bear.*

Speaking of his work, Bob says, "After all, bears come from the woods. Wood comes from the woods. And we all know Woody Bears come from the woods."

The enchanting faces of the Raikes bears were sculpted from "Oregon sugar pine," with high-quality synthetic fur bodies and jointed limbs. The bodies were stuffed with polyester fiberfill and had hand-carved wooden feet and paw pads.

The "Raikes Originals Woody Bear" certificate of authenticity accompanied each bear Robert Raikes produced. The number of that particular bear and the date it was made was hand-written on the certificate. This version of a certificate was used until 1986, when it appears it was changed in 1987. This is the original certificate for the Jester bear. Courtesy of Peter and Janice Spitzer.

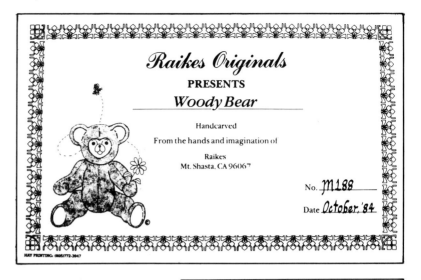

Example of the hand-tag that was attached to Robert Raikes' Woody Bears. Courtesy of Cathy and Robert Raikes Sr.

Jester. Woody Bear. *1984. A Robert Raikes original. 16in (41cm) tall; beige acrylic fur; hand-carved wooden face and foot pads; hand-painted face; inset plastic eyes; jointed arms and legs; swivel head; hard-stuffed body; hand-carved on foot "Raikes '84 M188." Dressed as a jester in pale and medium shades of lavender satin. Colors coordinate with painted face.*

With the success of Robert Raikes' clown dolls, it was only natural for him to create bears with hand-painted clown faces. Each bear came with its own certificate of authenticity. Courtesy of Peter and Janice Spitzer.

Woody Bear. *1984. A Robert Raikes original. 20in (50cm) tall; long dark brown acrylic fur; hand-carved wooden face and foot pads; inset plastic eyes; jointed arms and legs; swivel head; hard-stuffed body; hand-carved on foot "Raikes '84 L210." Dressed in gray, black and beige tweed vest, beige tie.*

Good example of one of the early hard-stuffed designs. Note how quickly Robert Raikes developed a very unique and professional look with his bears. It appears hand-carved wooden pads were only used on the feet on the early designs. Courtesy of Cathy and Robert Raikes Sr.

Woody Bear. *1984. A Robert Raikes original. 19in (48cm) tall; light beige acrylic fur; hand-carved wooden face and foot pads; inset plastic eyes; hand-painted freckles on snout; jointed arms and legs; hand-stuffed body; hand-carved on foot "Raikes '84 L280." Dressed in lavender and white apron and white bonnet.*

One of the earlier "hard-stuffed" designs. Courtesy of Molly Bakkum.

Woody Bear. *1984. A Robert Raikes original. Approximately 18in (46cm) tall; black acrylic fur; hand-carved wooden face and foot pads; inset plastic eyes; jointed arms and legs; swivel head; hard-stuffed body; signed and numbered on foot.*

Many of the early bears would be originally dressed with only a tie, bow or a bib. Photograph taken by Robert Raikes in the beautiful snow-covered mountains surrounding his Mount Shasta home. Courtesy of Robert and Carol Raikes.

Faerie. Woody Bear. *Circa 1984. A Robert Raikes original. Approximately 14in (36cm) tall; dark gray variegated acrylic fur; hand-carved wooden face, wings and foot pads; inset plastic eyes; jointed arms and legs; swivel head; hard-stuffed body; hand-signed and numbered on foot.*

Very few Raikes Faerie bears were produced. With Robert Raikes' uncanny ability to bring fantasy to a tangible state and the tremendous response he received from his Faerie dolls, it was only natural he should design a Faerie bear. Courtesy of Robert and Carol Raikes.

(Left) Woody Bear. *1984. A Robert Raikes original. 16in (41cm) tall; dark brown acrylic fur; hand-carved wooden face and foot pads; inset plastic eyes; hard-stuffed body; jointed arms and legs; swivel head; hand-carved on foot "Raikes '84 M119."*

Early "burned" wood method.

(Right) Woody Bear. *1984. A Robert Raikes original. 16in (41cm) tall; pale gray acrylic fur; hand-carved wooden face and foot pads; inset plastic eyes; hard-stuffed body; jointed arms and legs; swivel head; hand-carved on foot "Raikes '84 M207;" tag on leg "Raikes Original Woody Bear."*

Early versions of the popular Chelsea-face design. Courtesy of Peter and Janice Spitzer.

Woody Bear. *1984. A Robert Raikes original. 10in (25cm) tall; all hand-carved wood; inset plastic eyes; jointed arms and legs; swivel head.*

One-of-a-kind experimental bear. Courtesy of Carol and Robert Raikes.

Pouty-face Woody Bear. *1984. A Robert Raikes original. 12in (31cm) tall; beige acrylic fur; hand-carved wooden face and foot pads; hand-painted freckles and eyebrows; inset plastic eyes; jointed arms and legs; swivel head; hard-stuffed body; signed on foot.*

A good example of a Raikes popular "pouty-face" bear design. As a natural follow-up to the pouty-face dolls, Robert Raikes produced a number of different series of pouty-face bears from 1983 to 1988. Courtesy of Cathy and Robert Raikes Sr.

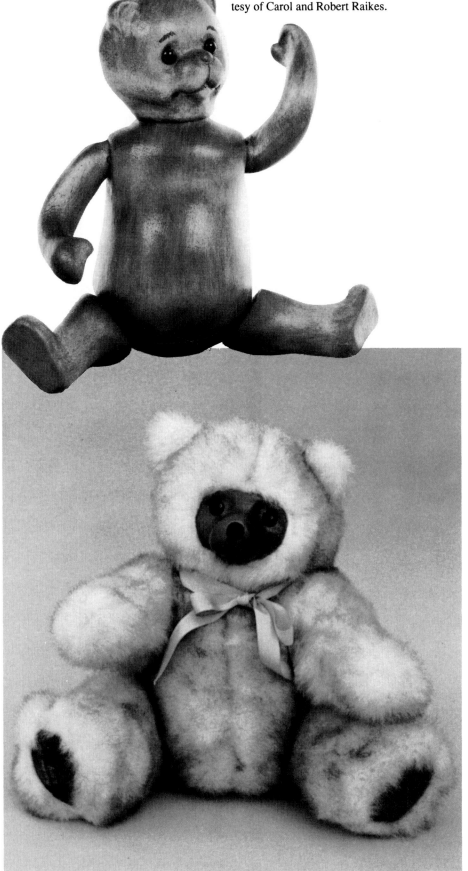

Woody Bear. *1984. A Robert Raikes original. 21in (53cm) tall; black-tipped silver acrylic fur; hand-carved wooden face and foot pads; inset plastic eyes; hand-stuffed body; jointed arms and legs; swivel head; hand-carved on foot "Raikes '84 L304."*

Note hand-carved and painted heart on left side of face. Courtesy of Peter and Janice Spitzer.

Masque-face Ballerina. Woody Bear. *1984. A Robert Raikes original. 18in (46cm) tall; variegated light beige acrylic fur; hand-carved wooden face and foot pads; hand-painted masque-face; inset plastic eyes; jointed arms and legs; swivel head; hard-stuffed body; signed, dated and numbered on foot. Dressed in pink tulle tutu with flower (at ear).*

Very popular design. Came in several face styles and fabric colors. Approximately 50 were produced. Photographed by Robert Raikes in Mount Shasta, California. Courtesy of Robert and Carol Raikes.

Jester. Woody Bear. *1984. A Robert Raikes original. Approximately 16in (41cm) tall; white acrylic fur; hand-carved wooden face and foot pads; inset plastic eyes; jointed arms and legs; swivel head; hand-signed, dated and numbered on foot. Dressed as a jester in a satin ruffle and hat.* Courtesy of Robert and Carol Raikes.

Tyrone *(Prototype)*. Woody Bear. *1984. A Robert Raikes original. 38in (97cm) tall; variegated gray acrylic fur; hand-carved wooden face, foot and paw pads; inset plastic eyes; jointed arms and legs; stationary head; hand-carved on foot "Raikes #1."*

When Bob decided to carve the prototype for Tyrone, *he could not find a piece of kiln-dried wood thick enough to carve the face. So he went into the woods with his chain saw and cut down a dead Port Orford cedar tree that was still standing. He sliced it down to the size he needed, blocked it out and then carved it. To allow the wood to dry faster, he hollowed the face out from behind. Bob's father is the proud owner of this rare and dignified fellow. He proudly sits in the half-scale Model T car Bob's father built in 1953 for the children to drive in their town's parade. Approximately 20* Tyrones *were produced between 1984 and 1986.* Courtesy of Cathy and Robert Raikes Sr.

An example of the progression of Robert Raikes original bears. On the right is one of his first designs with the flatter snout, applied hand-carved wooden nose and painted eyes (1982). On the left we see how this creative artist's work developed a design of a bear (made in 1985) that has established him the recognition of being one of America's best-known and successful teddy bear artists of the 1980s-1990s. Courtesy of Robert and Carol Raikes.

OPPOSITE PAGE: Robert Raikes' creative versions of a traditional Santa Claus have proven extremely popular editions among his collectors. The Santa on the right is a proto-type and the 54in (126cm) one-of-a-kind Santa in the background was produced by Bob for a Christmas display at his hometown mall in Tucson, Arizona, in 1991. Courtesy of Robert and Carol Raikes.

Santa. Woody Bear. 1984. A Robert Raikes original. Approximately 22in (56cm) tall; dark brown acrylic fur; hand-carved wooden face and foot pads; inset plastic eyes; spun glass beard; jointed arms and legs; swivel head; hand-signed, dated and numbered on foot.

Robert Raikes designed approximately four different designs of Santa bears. One was the size of Tyrone 36in (91cm) tall. Two were designs for Applause. Courtesy of Robert and Carol Raikes.

Swiss Girl. Woody Bear. *1985. A Robert Raikes original. 24in (56cm) tall; cream-colored acrylic fur; hand-carved wooden face, feet and paw pads; hand-painted paw design; inset plastic eyes; jointed arms and legs; swivel head; hand-carved on foot "Raikes LS079;" label on leg "Raikes Original Woody Bear." Dressed in red pinafore, white blouse and dark blue scarf.*

Rebecca-face. Note hand-carved wooden paw pads were now being used on a large percentage of the bears. Also, we see hand-painted foot design is added to some of the bears. This facial design was reproduced by Applause as Rebecca *in the first edition in 1985. The oil painting of Raikes'* Rebecca *by Applause is on canvas and was painted by Pat Woodman.* Courtesy of Robert and Pat Woodman. Photograph by Robert Woodman.

(Left) Jamie. Woody Bear. *1985. A Robert Raikes original. 11in (28cm) tall; brown acrylic fur; hand-carved wooden face and foot pads; hand-painted freckles on snout; inset plastic eyes; jointed arms and legs; swivel head; hand-written on foot in brown ink "41 Raikes '85."*
(Center) Jamie. Woody Bear. *1988. A Robert Raikes original. 12in (28cm) tall; tan wool; hand-carved wooden face and foot pads; hand-painted freckles on snout; inset plastic eyes; jointed arms and legs; swivel head; hand-written in brown ink "Robert Raikes 1988."*
(Right) Jamie. Woody Bear. *1985. A Robert Raikes original. 12in (28cm) tall; black variegated gray acrylic fur; hand-carved wooden face and foot pads; hand-painted freckles on snout; inset plastic eyes; jointed arms and legs; swivel head; hand-written on foot in brown ink "39 Raikes '85."*
Three versions of Robert Raikes' Jamie. Courtesy of Peter and Janice Spitzer.

However, the majority of the early designs did not have carved wooden paw pads. As the faces on the bears were carved, Bob felt the bodies should have more of a firm sculptured feeling. So he employed local high school football players to stuff the bodies. Bob changed this form of stuffing when the collectors requested he make the bodies softer and more cuddly."

The very first bears Bob made were quite primitive looking. At first, he experimented with carving most of the face including the ears (but not the nose) from one piece of wood, and then hand-painting the eyes. Unsure of how to carve the nose, Bob applied a separate sculptured small wood nose. This rare and interesting example of Raikes' first bear's head would not have been saved had it not been for Robert Raikes Sr., who retrieved it from the trash where his son had discarded it the day before.

The artist's next attempt (1981) was a personal project of a little unjointed, plush teddy bear. It was a Christmas gift for his mother in 1981. As before, he hand-carved a similar face, but this time made the ears of plush as part of the head.

Raikes made his first real serious teddy bear prototype in 1982. On page 46 we see a basic jointed teddy bear with the *Woody Bear* hand-carved wooden face starting to take shape.

The first design Bob made for resale had many of his experimental characteristics with the small applied sculptured nose. However, he changed the eyes to yellow plastic (not inset) and added hand-carved wooden foot pads. Produced in 1983, there were only approximately ten of this design.

Just as it was with his dolls, it was not long before the talented artist created a more professional and appealing-looking bear. He quickly mastered the problem with the nose by learning to carve the entire face from one piece of wood and insetting the eyes.

Bob improved upon another early method of work. Instead of burning the wood with a blowtorch to obtain the look he wanted, he was able to accomplish a realistic effect by allowing the natural grain of the wood to show through. After the features are carved, sanded and painted, the wood is finished with a clear protective coat. In some cases, a little pigment was added to the lacquer to give it color and depth. Freckles were also painted on the face and a stenciled foot design on the feet was an additional attraction on some of the bears.

Bob also experimented with carving in redwood, but found it a difficult medium in which to work, so there were very few of these bears made.

Every bear was hand-carved, signed, dated and numbered on the foot and came with its own certificate of authenticity. Most of the bears were signed "Robert Raikes," "R.W. Raikes" or "Raikes." Bob almost always hand-carved the identification marks and his signature, but in some instances he used a permanent ink pen. A percentage also came with a cloth tag sewn into the leg with the name "Raikes Original Woody Bear" on the label. In addition, the "Woody Bear, Raikes Originals" hang tag was tied

Woody Bear. 1985. A Robert Raikes original. 23in (58cm) tall; dark brown acrylic fur; hand-carved "redwood" face, feet and paws; inset plastic eyes; jointed arms and legs; swivel head; hand-carved on foot "Raikes '85 LS095."

Robert Raikes experimented by using redwood, but found it a difficult medium in which to work. He produced approximately two dolls in redwood, one of which was an Indian, and approximately 20 bears. Note the stenciled foot design. Courtesy of Peter and Janice Spitzer.

Panda. Woody Bear. 1985. A Robert Raikes original. 24in (61cm) tall; black and white acrylic fur; hand-carved wooden face, foot and paw pads; hand-painted face, foot and paw pads; inset plastic eyes; jointed arms and legs; swivel head; hand-carved on foot "1985 R. Raikes #3."

Robert Raikes produced several small editions of pandas with different faces. Courtesy of Cathy and Robert Raikes Sr.

(Left) Koala. Woody Bear. 1985. A Robert Raikes original. 15in (38cm) tall; gray and white acrylic fur; hand-carved wooden nose; black Ultrasuede foot and paw pads; inset plastic eyes; jointed arms and legs; swivel head.

One-of-a-kind experimental design. (Right) Koala. Woody Bear. 1986. A Robert Raikes original. 16in (41cm) tall; gray and white acrylic fur; hand-carved wooden nose, foot and paw pads; hand-painted black nose, foot and paw pads; plastic eyes; jointed arms and legs; swivel head; hand-carved on foot "85 Raikes 3."

Approximately 15 were produced of this koala design. At this writing, this is the only edition of koalas Robert Raikes produced. Courtesy of Cathy and Robert Raikes Sr.

59

Woody Bear. *1986. A Robert Raikes original.*
23in (58cm) tall; snowy white silky acrylic
fur; hand-carved wooden face, feet and paw
pads; hand-painted foot design; inset plastic
eyes; jointed arms and legs; swivel head; hand-
carved on foot "Raikes 1986 Robert Raikes 1-
25;" label on leg "Raikes Original Woody
Bear."

The hand-painted mask on the face adds
so much character to the bear. Courtesy of
Peter and Janice Spitzer.

Woody Bear. *1985. A Robert Raikes original.*
18in (46cm) tall; variegated dark gray acrylic
fur; hand-carved wooden face, foot and paw
pads; inset plastic eyes; jointed arms and legs;
swivel head; hand-carved on foot "Raikes
MS064;" hand-signed in black ink "Robert
Raikes 1985."

Note Chelsea-*face. This facial design was*
reproduced by Applause as Chelsea *in the first*
edition in 1985. Courtesy of Colleen Fontana.

Six months of hard work are shown here in
the Raikes hand-carved heads awaiting to be
assembled into adorable Woody Bears. *Cour-*
tesy of Robert and Carol Raikes.

to the arm of the bear. Each bear was an original. However, the bears were made in a series of limited editions.

The majority of the editions were limited to 25 or 30. Unless there was a special one-of-a-kind bear or a prototype, most of the bears were numbered.

Originally, they were hand-signed, dated and numbered in black ink. It appears the numbers did not signify the number of the bears made as approximately only ten of this early design were produced. Also marked on the bear's foot were the letters indicating the size: "T.B.," "S.B.," "M.B." or "B.B.," meaning tiny, small, medium or big bear. With the introduction of a new design where the bear's face was now carved entirely from one piece of wood, the identification system changed. For example, "Raikes '84 M188." This indicated the bear was medium size, number 188, made in 1984. In approximately 1985, when the "firm" stuffing of the bears was changed to the "soft," more cuddly variety, the letters were changed slightly to "SS," "MS" or "LS," which simply implied the body now had soft stuffing. For example, "Raikes MS032 '85" indicated the bear was medium size, softly stuffed, number 32, made in 1985.

As I stated earlier, the majority of the bears were made in editions. In 1986, the identification system was changed yet again, to inform the collectors of the number in the edition of that particular bear. The letters indicating the size "SS," "MS" and "LS" were deleted. Now the bears were marked with the edition as well as the number of that specific bear. For example, "Raikes 7/25 '86" clearly informed the collector this bear was number seven in an edition of 25 made in 1986.

The only problem with the numbering system that concerned Bob was the collectors might not realize each bear was an original piece, only similar within the series. Take for example, the *Ballerina*. All were dressed like ballerinas with painted faces, but each bear's clothes and face were slightly modified.

The popularity of the bears increased to such an extent that soon the Raikes stopped producing so many dolls and concentrated on creating teddy bears.

Bob and Carol were already working long hours on the dolls. So, when they decided to produce bears, Bob approached his brother, Mike, and his wife, Cindy, with the idea of helping with the bears in their spare time, on a "profit sharing" basis. Mike was a wood shop teacher at Mount Shasta High School, and the "profit sharing" agreement made sense to him.

Mike assembled the parts and stuffed the bears after Cindy made the bodies. Bob told the humorous story of how his brother's house soon began to resemble his own as he was initiated into the *Woody Bear* business. "There he was, with a whole room stuffed full of fur and polyfill, stuffing 'Woodies' like mad every night till midnight," Bob said laughingly. It is difficult at first for anyone to comprehend the terrific amount of energy that goes into a project like this.

Panda. Woody Bear. *1986. A Robert Raikes original. 24in (61cm) tall; silky black and white acrylic fur; hand-carved wooden face, feet and paw pads; hand-painted black and white face; inset plastic eyes; jointed arms and legs; swivel head; hand-carved on foot "R.W. Raikes 1986 #7"; hand-signed in gold ink "Robert Raikes."*

Several small editions of Raikes' pandas were produced with different faces. This panda was the second design made. Courtesy of Peter and Janice Spitzer.

Baby Woody Bears. *Circa 1986. A Robert Raikes original. Approximately 12in (31cm) tall; (Left) beige acrylic fur; (Right) dark brown acrylic fur; Ultrasuede inner ears, foot and paw pads; hand-carved wooden snout; hand-painted freckles and features; plastic eyes; jointed arms and legs; stationary head.*

Experimental bears. Approximately four or five different versions of Raikes' Baby Woody Bears were produced in very small editions. Courtesy of Robert and Carol Raikes.

(Left) Woody Bear. *1986. A Robert Raikes original. 18in (46cm) tall; black acrylic fur; hand-carved face, feet and foot pads; inset plastic eyes; jointed arms and legs; swivel head; hand-carved on foot "4/25 Raikes 1986." Dressed in pink and white "party dress" with matching bow (at ear).*

Note Chelsea-*face. Another edition of this popular sweet-face design.*
(Middle Left) Pouty-face *Ballerina. Woody Bear. 1985. A Robert Raikes original. 18in (46cm) tall; cream-colored acrylic fur; hand-carved wooden face, feet and paw pads; inset plastic eyes; jointed arms and legs; swivel head; hand-carved on foot "Raikes '85 MS032." Dressed in pink tulle tutu and pink rose (at ear).*

Outfits were also available in pastel shades of mint green, lavender and yellow.
(Middle Right) Sailor. Woody Bear. *1985. A Robert Raikes original. 18in (46cm) tall; brown acrylic fur; hand-carved wooden face, feet and paw pads; hand-painted freckles on snout; inset plastic eyes; jointed arms and legs; swivel head; hand-carved on foot "Raikes '85 MS 028." Dressed in white and blue sailor suit.*
(Right) Pouty-face *Woody Bear. 1986. A Robert Raikes original. 18in (46cm) tall; snowy white acrylic fur; hand-carved face, feet and paws; inset plastic eyes; jointed arms and legs; swivel head; hand-carved on foot "Robert Raikes 2/25 1986." Dressed in knitted dark blue and white scarf and hat, with the words "Woody Bear" knitted into scarf.*

Example of the four outfits the 18in (46cm) tall original Raikes Woody Bears *were dressed in during 1985 to 1986.* Courtesy of Peter and Janice Spitzer.

Baby Bear. Woody Bear. *1986. A Robert Raikes original. 16in (41cm) tall; pale cinnamon-colored acrylic fur; pale beige Ultrasuede inner ears; hand-carved wooden face, feet and paw pads; inset plastic eyes; jointed arms and legs; swivel head; hand-carved on foot "R.W. Raikes 1986 #5."*

Baby Bear was originally created in celebration of Linda Mullins' 1986 San Diego Teddy Bear, Doll and Antique Toy Festival where Robert Raikes appeared as a celebrity guest. Approximately 21 were in the edition. A small percentage had cry boxes encased in body. They came in a variety of colors and furs. Some had hand-painted freckles on face. Note the unusual design of the carved wooden face and chunky baby body. Courtesy of Francine Ferris.

(Left) Swiss Girl. Woody Bear. 1986. A Robert Raikes original. 23in (58cm) tall; dark brown acrylic fur; hand-carved wooden face, feet and paw pads; hand-painted foot design and freckles on snout; inset plastic eyes; jointed arms and legs; swivel head; hand-carved on foot "Raikes '86 14-25;" label on leg "Raikes Original Woody Bear." Dressed in maroon dress and scarf, white blouse, maroon and white print apron.

(Center) Ballerina. Woody Bear. 1987. A Robert Raikes original. 23in (58.4cm) tall; snowy white acrylic fur; hand-carved wooden face (smiling), feet and paw pads; hand-painted freckles on face and foot design; inset plastic eyes; jointed arms and legs; swivel head; hand-carved on foot "1987 Robert Raikes 14/25." Dressed in pink tulle tutu and pink rose (at ear).

(Right) Country Girl. Woody Bear. 1986. A Robert Raikes original. 23.5in (60cm) tall; black acrylic fur; hand-carved wooden face, feet and paw pads; hand-painted freckles and foot design; inset plastic eyes; jointed arms and legs; swivel head; hand-carved on foot "'86 Raikes 11/25;" label on leg "Raikes Original Woody Bear." Dressed in blue and pink print dress and matching bonnet, white apron.

Example of the outfits in which Raikes 23in (58cm) tall girl bears were dressed during 1987 to 1988. Courtesy of Peter and Janice Spitzer.

Tyrone. Woody Bear. 1986. A Robert Raikes original. 38in (97cm) tall; pale gray acrylic fur; hand-carved wooden face, feet and paw pads; inset plastic eyes; jointed arms and legs; stationary head; hand-carved on foot "'86 Raikes #13."

Note dark effect given to wood. Rare Scotsman outfit. The majority of Tyrones are dressed in tuxedos. Courtesy of Peter and Janice Spitzer.

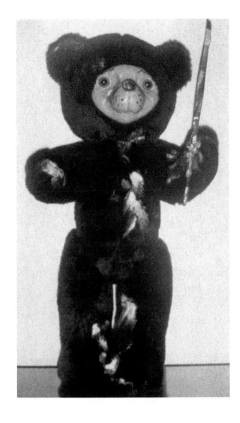

The Artist Woody Bear was one of Bob's favorites. He said he had fun smearing different colors of paint over parts of the fir. Circa 1987. 15in (38cm) tall. Approximately four Raikes' Artist bears were produced. Courtesy of Robert and Carol Raikes.

Bob was constantly working on new and original designs. The public response to Raikes' *Woody Bears* was nothing short of sensational. His fame spread fast, establishing him as one of America's best-known and respected original teddy bear artists and sculptors of the 1980s.

When asked if he felt his bears were people, Bob replied, "Bears are bears and people are people. Rather, I see them as extensions of our personalities. In that respect I think they are mirrors of our humanity. In the same way a child wants a teddy bear for warmth and security, adults find in teddy bears reflections of the better nature of man...for adults, something very important to hold onto."

As with his dolls, the creative artist made numerous appealing designs of bears.

As a natural follow-up to the pouty face dolls, Bob produced a series of pouty-face bears. Another popular design was the *Ballerina* bear. They came in several face styles and fabric colors. They were dressed in dainty tulle tutus and flower (at ear). These outfits were available in pastel shades of mint green, lavender, rose and yellow. Bob's favorite was a 24in (61cm) *Pouty Ballerina* bear in white plush with a pink tutu.

In 1985, Bob experimented with several koala faces. There were approximately only 15 made.

There were several small editions of pandas with different faces. The painted black and white faces were all extremely striking. He also made one impressive looking panda the size of *Tyrone*, 38in (97cm) tall.

The *Artist* was another of his favorites. "I only made about four *Artist* bears, but they were fun to make, as I smeared different colored paint over parts of the plush."

Bob experimented with making *Santa Bears*. Here again only four designs were made. One was quite large and came with a spun glass beard.

Very popular and quite rare were Bob's *Pirates*. He made about ten between 1984 and 1986. They came with a hook in place of one paw and a patch over the right eye.

When Bob created the prototype for his 38in (97cm) tall *Tyrone*, he could not find a piece of kiln-dried wood thick enough to carve the face. So he went into the woods with his chain saw and cut down a dead Port Orford cedar tree that was still standing. He sliced it down to the size he needed, blocked it out and then carved it. To allow the wood to dry faster, he hollowed the face out from behind.

Bob's father is the proud owner of this rare and dignified-looking fellow. He recalls the attention the bear would receive when he took him to shows for exhibit,

(Left) Boy. Woody Bear. *1987. A Robert Raikes original. 23in (58cm) tall; light beige acrylic fur; hand-carved wooden face, feet and paw pads; hand-painted foot design; inset plastic eyes; jointed arms and legs; swivel head; hand-carved on foot "Robert Raikes 1987 24/25." Dressed in brown check waistcoat with beige tie. (Center) Girl.* Woody Bear. *1987. A Robert Raikes original. 23in (58cm) tall; dark brown acrylic fur; hand-carved wooden face, feet and paw pads; hand-painted foot design; inset plastic eyes; jointed arms and legs; swivel head; hand-carved on foot "Robert Raikes 6/25 1987." Dressed in pink and white striped dress with white cotton pinafore. (Right) Pouty-face Boy.* Woody Bear. *1986. A Robert Raikes original. 22in (56cm) tall; snowy white acrylic fur; hand-carved wooden face, feet and paw pads; inset plastic eyes; jointed arms and legs; swivel head; hand-carved on foot "Raikes 14/25 '86." Dressed in black velvet tuxedo, white shirt, white satin vest and black bow tie. Courtesy of Peter and Janice Spitzer.*

(Left) Train Engineer. Woody Bear. *1987. A Robert Raikes original. 22in (56cm) tall; variegated black and gray acrylic fur; hand-painted freckles on snout and foot design; inset plastic eyes; jointed arms and legs; swivel head; hand-carved on foot "Robert Raikes 1987 5/25." Dressed in blue and white striped engineer overalls and cap, red and white scarf.*
(Center) Country Boy. Woody Bear. *1986. A Robert Raikes original. 23in (58cm) tall; pale beige acrylic fur; hand-carved wooden face, feet and paw pads; hand-painted freckles and foot design; inset plastic eyes; jointed arms and legs; swivel head; hand-carved on foot "R W Raikes 1986½s"; label on leg "Raikes Original Woody Bear." Dressed in blue denim overalls and pale blue shirt.*

This design of face was reproduced by Applause as Sebastian *in their first edition in 1985.*
(Right) Swiss Boy. Woody Bear. *1986. A Robert Raikes original. 23in (58cm) tall; brown and variegated beige acrylic fur; hand-carved wooden face, feet and paw pads; hand-painted freckles and foot design; inset plastic eyes; jointed arms and legs; swivel head; hand-written in gold ink on foot "1986 Robert Raikes 7-25." Dressed in brown lederhosen and white shirt.* Courtesy of Peter and Janice Spitzer.

It appears this Robert Raikes certificate of authenticity was introduced in 1987 and was used for the Raikes dolls and the Woody Bears. Courtesy of Peter and Janice Spitzer.

Sherwood. Woody Bear. *1987. A Robert Raikes original. 18in (46cm) tall; short black acrylic fur; hand-carved wooden face and foot pads; inset plastic eyes; jointed arms and legs; swivel head; hand-carved on foot "Robert Raikes 1987 25/25."*

A later version of Raikes' popular Sherwood *design. Note no hand-carved wooden paw pads are used on* Sherwood. Courtesy of Robert and Pat Woodman. Photograph by Robert Woodman.

A Robert Raikes
Original
created for you

"A little joy and a smile
May my creations bring to you
And much more . . .
For me the happiness of knowing
We have shared a dream or two."

Name
Number
Date

Robert Raikes

Ballerina. Woody Bear. *1987. A Robert Raikes original. 20in (51cm) tall; white acrylic fur; hand-carved wooden face, feet and paw pads; inset plastic eyes; jointed arms and legs; swivel head; signed on foot. Dressed in pink tulle tutu and flower (at ear).*

This is the only Ballerina Robert Raikes made with this facial design. It is also one of the artist's favorite bears. Courtesy of Robert and Carol Raikes.

Joey. Woody Bear. *1987. A Robert Raikes original. 12in (31cm) tall; short light brown acrylic fur; hand-carved wooden face and foot pads; inset plastic eyes; unjointed arms and legs; stationary head; hand-carved on foot "1987 Robert Raikes 5-50." Courtesy of Robert and Pat Woodman. Photograph by Robert Woodman.*

Masque-face. Woody Bear. *1987. A Robert Raikes original. 60in (152cm) tall; black acrylic fur; hand-carved wooden face, feet and paw pads; hand-painted foot and paw designs on pads; hand-painted clown face; inset plastic eyes; jointed arms and legs; swivel head; hand-carved on foot "Robert Raikes;" numbered on certificate "1 of 1." Dressed in dark green velvet jacket with gold lame collar and silver lame bow tie.*

One-of-a-kind. Beautiful hand-painted face. Courtesy of Gene Zion.

Kevi. Woody Bear. *1987. A Robert Raikes original. 14in (36cm) tall; golden brown acrylic fur; hand-carved wooden face and foot pads; hand-painted eyes; unjointed arms and legs; stationary head; hand-signed and numbered on foot.*

The concept for the Kevi bear came to Bob after he had met the internationally acclaimed singer and entertainer Kevin Roth. Bob was so impressed by the children's response to Kevin and his singing that he had the idea to make a bear with a tape recording of Kevin's singing accompanying the bear. Applause reproduced the original Raikes Kevi bear with a tape recording of Kevin Roth singing. However, Raikes' original Kevi does not include a tape. Courtesy of Robert and Carol Raikes.

(Top left) Girl. Woody Bear. 1987. A Robert Raikes original. 17in (43cm) tall; long cream-colored acrylic fur; hand-carved wooden face, feet and paw pads; inset plastic eyes; jointed arms and legs; swivel head; hand-carved on foot "Robert Raikes 1987 17-25." Dressed in white and lavender nightdress and mop cap.

(Top right) Girl. Woody Bear. 1988. A Robert Raikes original. 17in (43cm) tall; variegated brown acrylic fur; hand-carved wooden face, feet and paw pads; jointed arms and legs; swivel head; hand-written in brown ink "1988 Robert Raikes 12/25." Dressed in blue pinafore with blue and white blouse with matching bow (at ear). Chelsea-face.

(Bottom left) Boy. Woody Bear. 1987. A Robert Raikes original. 18in (46cm) tall; long cream-colored acrylic fur; hand-carved wooden face, feet and paw pads; inset plastic eyes; jointed arms and legs; swivel head; hand-carved on foot "Robert Raikes 1987 7-25." Dressed in brown wool pants, white shirt and brown bow tie.

(Bottom center) Boy. Woody Bear. 1987. A Robert Raikes original. 18in (46cm) tall; long gray and black variegated acrylic fur; hand-carved wooden face, feet and paw pads; hand-painted freckles on snout; inset plastic eyes; jointed arms and legs; swivel head; hand-carved on foot "R.Raikes 1987 8/25." Dressed in gray and black flecked vest with rust-colored tie.

(Bottom right) Girl. Woody Bear. 1988. A Robert Raikes original. 17in (43cm) tall; light gray acrylic fur; hand-carved wooden face, feet and paw pads; hand-painted freckles on snout; inset plastic eyes; jointed arms and legs; swivel head; hand-carved on foot "1988 Robert Raikes 12-25." Dressed as a Swiss baby girl in a maroon dress with white lace bonnet.

Example of the outfits in which the 17in (43cm) tall bears were dressed in during 1987 and 1988. Courtesy of Peter and Janice Spitzer.

Mother's Day (Prototype). Woody Bear. 1988. A Robert Raikes original. 17in (42cm) tall; light beige acrylic fur; hand-carved wooden face, feet and paw pads; inset plastic eyes; jointed arms and legs; swivel head; hand-signed in brown ink "Robert Raikes' Mother's Day Prototype."

Heart-shaped face with hand-painted freckles. Dressed in rose pink and floral dress and bow (at ear). Applause reproduced Raikes' Mother's Day bear in 1989. Courtesy of Peter and Janice Spitzer.

Sherwood. Woody Bear. 1987. A Robert Raikes original. 16in (41cm) tall; beige acrylic fur; hand-carved wooden face and foot pads; hand-painted freckles on snout; inset plastic eyes; jointed arms and legs; swivel head;

Experimental design of Sherwood. Courtesy of Peter and Janice Spitzer.

Miniature Woody Bears. *1988. A Robert Raikes original. 8in (20cm) tall; various shades of brown acrylic fur; hand-carved wooden face and foot pads; hand-painted eyes and features; jointed arms and legs; swivel head; signed on foot.*

Experimental bears. Approximately ten were made. Note seated bear has felt foot pads. Courtesy of Robert and Carol Raikes.

Faerie Rabbit. *1984. A Robert Raikes original. 19in (48cm) tall; all hand-carved wood; articulated head and body; hand-painted body and features; whiskers; hand-signed and dated. Dressed as a faerie in rose-colored leaf-shaped silk flowers.*

The highly collectible and very rare Faerie Rabbits *are fine examples of the detail and creativity of Robert Raikes' work. Note the hand-painted body.* Courtesy of Robert and Carol Raikes.

(Left) Emily. Woody Bear. *1988. A Robert Raikes original. 24in (61cm) tall; light gray acrylic fur; hand-carved wooden face, feet and paw pads; inset plastic eyes; jointed arms and legs; swivel head; hand-carved on foot "1988 Robert Raikes 11-30." Attired in pink print dress with pale pink collar. Dress varies throughout the edition.*
(Center) Jason. Woody Bear. *1988. A Robert Raikes original. 18in (46cm) tall; beige acrylic fur; hand-carved wooden face, feet and paw pads; inset plastic eyes; jointed arms and legs; swivel head; hand-carved on foot "1988 Robert Raikes 21-25." Dressed in a hand-knitted sweater, velvet cap and bow tie.*

(Right) Jenny (Prototype). Woody Bear. *1988. A Robert Raikes original. 18in (46cm) tall; beige acrylic fur; jointed arms and legs; swivel head; hand-carved on foot "1988 Robert Raikes Prototype." Outfitted in rust-colored dress with matching bow (at ear).*

Emily, Jason *and* Jenny *were named after Robert Raikes' children. They were reproduced by Applause in the summer of 1988 sixth edition as the "Home Sweet Home Collection."* Courtesy of Peter and Janice Spitzer.

68

especially when he would drive up with *Tyrone* riding in the front seat of the car. Now the bear is retired and has a place of honor in the Raikes Sr.'s home. He proudly sits in the half-scaled Model T car Bob's father built in 1953 for the children to drive in their town's parades.

I asked Bob what gives him ideas for his various characters. He smiled and replied, "Many of my designs represent my childhood memories. Growing up in the late 1950s and early 60s, I loved watching cowboy and Indian movies. Two of my favorite stars were Roy Rogers and Dale Evans. That is where the idea for Bonnie and Jesse (the cowgirl and cowboy I designed for Applause) came from.

"Then there was Engineer Bill. I feel my Train Engineer was a perfect interpretation of that popular celebrity and proved to be one of my most popular designs. I produced a few at a time between 1984 and 1988. I always varied the faces and the plush. And each engineer came with a train logo."

The concept for the *Kevi* bear came to Bob after he had met the internationally acclaimed singer and entertainer Kevin Roth at the Hobby Center Toys, Doll and Teddy Bear Show in Toledo, Ohio. Bob was so impressed by the children's response to Kevin and his singing that Bob conceived the idea to make a bear with a tape recording of Kevin's singing accompanying the bear. After the show, Bob was at the airport waiting for his plane to arrive and he began to draw a couple of sketches of the *Kevi* bear. He said he was so excited about the idea, he could hardly wait to get to his studio the next morning to begin work on the prototype.

The idea for the painted-face clown dolls and bears originally came to be by unusual circumstances. Bob found a small imperfection or coloration in the wood on the face of a doll so rather than discard the piece, he came up with the notion to paint a design into that section, then make it symmetrical on the other side. The finished product was so stunning, and the creative artist so enjoyed the challenge of something new, that he produced a variety of clown dolls and small editions of clown bears between 1977 and 1986. On those *Ballerina* and *Jester* bears with slight discoloration in the wood, Bob would also artistically paint beautiful colored masks.

Many of the names the artist chose for his bears were taken from the children of his secretary, seamstress and various friends. Bob suddenly realized he had never named his bears after any of his own children. So the bears in the Applause "Home Sweet Home Collection" and Raikes originals of these designs were given his children's names, Jenny, Jason, and Emily.

Over the years, Bob also created variations of beautiful rabbits—all hand-carved wood fairy rabbits, all hand-carved wood articulated rabbits and plush rabbits in many sizes. These wonderful rabbits proved to be so popular, Bob went on to create many other outstanding animals.

Among Raikes' intriguing menagerie creations were hedgehogs, raccoons, owls and pigs.

Four different designs of pigs were produced. The first pig was 26in (66cm) tall and unusual in that it had jointed arms, but the body consisted of a square solid block of wood. A long country-style dress concealed the block body. Because of its design, it was very stable and could be used as a doorstop.

The next pig Bob designed was a 6in (15cm) tall character wearing a country dress. In 1987, he introduced an edition of 23in (58cm) tall pigs. They came in pairs dressed as a boy and girl. There were approximately 20 pairs in this edition.

There was only one style of hedgehog made. Dressed to look like a princess, she was designed to go with *Robin Raccoon*. However, they were sold separately. The hedgehog and the raccoon were made in an edition of 50 each.

To date, Bob has produced about 40 owls, 24 monkeys, 50 beavers and 50 bunnies. All the animals had jointed arms and legs and stationary heads, with the exception of the monkey. He was completely jointed with a poseable tail.

Although the Raikes had a thriving and successful bear-making business, Bob found he could not keep up the demand of his one-of-a-kind bears. Creating over 1200 original designs and exhibiting at 32 shows a year, he was already working at top production speed.

It was then he made the decision to approach the major gift company, Applause, to produce his designs. In the agreement, Bob was still able to produced special order bears under the name *Woody Bear*. However, on Bob's 40th birthday, October 13, 1987, the artist made the decision that a good portion of his original work will be produced for charitable organizations, special events and for members of the Robert Raikes Collector's Club. Since that time, his already valuable pieces have increased in value tremendously and are still climbing and extremely scarce.

Winged Faerie Rabbit. *1984. A Robert Raikes original. 10in (25cm) tall; all hand-carved wood; articulated head and body; hand-painted features; hand-signed and dated. Dressed as a faerie with gold wings and silk outfit in the shape of leaves.* Courtesy of Cathy and Robert Raikes Sr.

Faerie Rabbit. *1984. A Robert Raikes original. 19in (48cm) tall; all hand-carved wood; articulated head and body; hand-painted features; whiskers; silk flower collar; hand-signed and dated.*

Approximately four of this design were produced. Courtesy of Robert and Carol Raikes.

Bride and Groom. *Rabbits. 1984. Robert Raikes originals. 21in (53cm) tall; all hand-carved wood; articulated heads and bodies; hand-painted features; whiskers; hand-written on foot in black ink "R W Raikes '84." Dressed as a bride and groom.*

Only one set of the rabbits dressed as a bride and groom was produced. Courtesy of Cathy and Robert Raikes Sr.

An example of the all hand-carved wood, articulated head and body used for the Raikes Faerie Rabbits. A percentage of the rabbits were of natural wood and a few had painted bodies. Courtesy of Robert and Carol Raikes.

Rabbits. 1984. Robert Raikes originals. Approximately 21in (53cm) tall; all hand-carved wood; articulated heads and bodies; hand-painted eyes and features; whiskers; hand-signed. Dressed as a boy and girl.

Sold in sets. Approximately 20 in edition. Courtesy of Robert and Carol Raikes.

Rabbits. 1986. Robert Raikes originals. 23in (58cm) tall; light beige acrylic fur; hand-carved wooden faces; sculptured beige Ultrasuede foot and paw pads; hand-painted eyes; whiskers; jointed arms and legs; swivel head; signed, dated and numbered in ink on foot. Girl dressed in pink dress with floral pinafore and pink bow (at ear). Boy dressed in black velvet vest and bow tie.

Note these rabbits have jointed heads. The first Applause "plush" rabbits. (Jill and Andrew) were made from this design. Courtesy of Robert and Carol Raikes.

Rabbit. 1986. A Robert Raikes original. 21in (53cm) tall; green acrylic fur; gray Ultrasuede inner ears, foot and paw pads; hand-carved wooden face; hand-painted eyes; whiskers, jointed arms and legs; stationary head; hand-written in ink "Raikes '86." Dressed in a smart green velvet waistcoat with red silk rose on lapel.

It appears this was the first design of Raikes' plush rabbits made for resale. Note the stationary head. The majority of the heads of Raikes' animals (excluding bears) were stationary. Courtesy of Peter and Janice Spitzer.

Rabbit. 1987. A Robert Raikes original. 24in (61cm) tall; pink acrylic fur; cream-colored Ultrasuede inner ears, foot and paw pads; hand-carved wooden face; hand-painted eyes; whiskers; jointed arms and legs; stationary head; hand-signed in black ink "1987 Raikes."

One-of-a-kind. Courtesy of Peter and Janice Spitzer.

(Left) Rabbit. 1986. A Robert Raikes original. 21in (53cm) tall; short gray acrylic fur; Ultrasuede inner ear, foot and paw pads; hand-carved wooden face; hand-painted eyes; jointed arms and legs; stationary head.

This design was used for the first edition of plush rabbits Robert Raikes produced. (Right) Rabbit. 1985. A Robert Raikes original. 15in (38cm) tall; long silky beige acrylic fur; beige Ultrasuede inner ear, foot and paw pads; hand-carved wooden face; hand-painted eyes; jointed arms and legs; stationary head.

First experimental design of a Raikes plush rabbit. Courtesy of Cathy and Robert Raikes Sr.

This is the first pig Bob designed. It stands 26in (66cm) tall and is unusual in that it has jointed arms, but the body consists of a square solid block of wood. The long country-style dress conceals the block body. Because of its design, it is very stable and can be used as a doorstop. Courtesy of Robert and Carol Raikes.

Dog. 1985. A Robert Raikes original. 12in (31cm) tall; short brown acrylic fur; hand-carved wooden face, foot and paw pads; hand-painted foot and paw pads design; inset plastic eyes; jointed arms and legs; stationary head; carved wooden bone; hand-signed.

Robert Raikes has created several designs of dogs in very small editions. However, this dog is a one-of-a-kind and at this writing, it has never been reproduced. Courtesy of Robert and Carol Raikes.

Original animals by Robert Raikes. 1985. Sizes range from 16in (41cm) tall to 20in (51cm) tall; various colors of acrylic fur; hand-carved faces.

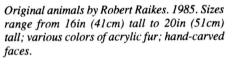

These were the prototypes of an experimental group of animals. The clothes were made by Applause. Courtesy of Robert and Carol Raikes.

Bunny. 1987. A Robert Raikes original. 9in (22cm) tall; pale beige acrylic fur; cream-colored Ultrasuede inner ears, foot and paw pads; hand-carved wooden face; hand-painted eyes; jointed arms and legs; stationary head; hand-signed in black ink "1987 Raikes 1-50." Courtesy of Peter and Janice Spitzer.

(Left) Hedgehog. 1987. A Robert Raikes original. 15in (38cm) tall; variegated brown acrylic fur; hand-carved wooden face, paws and feet; inset plastic eyes; hand-painted features; jointed arms and legs; stationary head; hand-carved on foot "Robert Raikes 1987 1-50."

Originally produced wearing a dress and cape.

(Center) Beaver. 1987. A Robert Raikes original. 16in (41cm) tall; dark brown acrylic fur; brown Ultrasuede tail and inner ear; hand-carved wooden face, teeth, paws and feet; inset plastic eyes; hand-painted features; jointed arms and legs, stationary head; hand-carved on foot "Robert Raikes 1987 13-50."

Originally produced with a matching jacket and hat.

(Right) Owl (Prototype). 1987. A Robert Raikes original. 12in (31cm) tall; variegated brown and white acrylic fur; hand-carved wooden face, beak and feet; inset plastic eyes; hand-painted features; jointed arms and legs; stationary head; hand-written on hang-tag "May 1987."

At this writing, the beaver, hedgehog and raccoon have been reproduced by Applause. Courtesy of Cathy and Robert Raikes Sr.

Monkey. 1987. A Robert Raikes original. 23in (58cm) tall; black acrylic fur; hand-carved wooden face, feet and hands; hand-painted brown eyes; jointed arms and legs; swivel head; poseable tail; hand-carved on foot "1987 Robert Raikes 3-24." Courtesy of Peter and Janice Spitzer.

Pigs. 1987. Robert Raikes originals. 23in (58cm) tall. Boy: short beige acrylic fur; light beige Ultrasuede inner ears; hand-carved wooden face and hooves; hand-painted brown eyes; jointed arms and legs; stationary head; hand-written on hoof in black ink "Robert Raikes #1 1987." Dressed in brown check pants, white shirt, brown waistcoat, brown check cap and bow tie. Girl: short pink acrylic fur; pale pink Ultrasuede in inner ears; hand-carved wooden face and hooves; hand-painted blue eyes; jointed arms and legs; stationary head; hand-signed in black ink on hoof "Robert Raikes #1 1987." Dressed in blue and white print blouse, pink and white striped skirt and apron, blue vest and pink mop cap.

Edition of 20 pairs. Robert Raikes produced four different designs of pigs. Courtesy of Peter and Janice Spitzer.

An extremely popular style of Raikes creations are the bears with the beautiful hand-painted faces. This 1991 Robert Raikes original is 24in (61cm) tall, produced in snowy white mohair and has an adorable hand-carved bee affixed to her ear. Courtesy Michael and Cayle Swindler.

Cat. 1989. A Robert Raikes original. 20in (51cm) tall; short pale cinnamon acrylic fur; hand-carved wooden face; Ultrasuede foot pads; inset green plastic eyes; jointed arms and legs; swivel head; hand-signed in black ink "Robert Raikes 4/49 1989."

Dressed in turquoise dress with yellow print sleeves, matching hat and pink apron. Courtesy of Robert and Pat Woodman. Photograph by Robert Woodman.

Chapter Five

Robert Raikes' Designs Find a Home With Applause

Applause, a world leader in the gift industry, is home to some of the best-known merchandising licenses in the country. The Woodland Hills, California based company holds the rights to popular characters from Disney, Sesame Street, Warner Bros. (Looney Tunes and Tiny Toons), Babar and many more. More than 50,000 retailers nationwide purchase some of the most recognizable gift merchandise in the country from this thriving, privately-held company.

The Wallace Berrie Company was founded in 1964 by Wallace Berrie, a manufacturer of drugstore novelty items. Growth was slow but steady until the mid-1970s when the mailman delivered a "little blue character about three apples tall." Unaware that other companies had turned down the property, Wallace Berrie aggressively sought worldwide rights to what became the Smurfs. The company created a sales phenomenon that sold over $1 billion in merchandise and was soon on the road to becoming a leader in the licensing industry.

In 1982, Wallace Berrie acquired the Applause Company from Knickerbocker Toys, picking up a number of classic licenses such as Disney, Sesame Street and Raggedy Ann and Andy. In 1986, the company changed its name to Applause and solidified its strength in both the gift and licensing areas by introducing the California Raisins.

Today, Applause, Inc. has expanded into many divisions. Applause Gift dominates the plush figurine, figurine and infant/toddler product categories of the gift industry. It is also a formidable presence in the ceramic home decor, collectible and alternative greeting card businesses. These divisions are marketed by one of the largest direct sales forces in the U.S. gift industry.

Applause Toys develops licensed and branded products for the mass market, while the company's International division markets the Applause product line through distributors in more than 45 countries.

The relationship between Bob Raikes and Applause all started with a Raikes letter and photos originally sent to Coleco which eventually found its way to Applause. A phone conversation ensued, and when Applause discovered Bob's parents were showing his work in Los Angeles, they made arrangements to have Robert Raikes Sr. and his wife, Cathy, come to their head office in Woodland Hills and show their son's work to Applause executives. The executives were so impressed, they purchased $2000 worth of Raikes items.

Applause showed the creations to three focus groups—doll collectors, gift retailers and collector stores—and met with fantastic reaction. The company then signed a contract agreement with Bob Raikes, and development began in January of 1985.

Raikes Bears were formally launched at the Los Angeles Gift Show (July 1985) with the media enthralled with Bob's carved samples. That first series sold out in 30 days. Since that time, Applause has grown five-fold and so has Bob's creations including limited edition musicals and snowdomes.

With Applause, Raikes can be sold to true collectors and be represented by a company with a reputation for collectibility.

It is an interesting study to follow a Raikes prototype from start to an Applause finished product:

1. First, the prototype is sent to the Orient with instructions concerning the clothing and type of plush to be used.

2. Then, the applause vendor makes a duplicate which is sent to Robert Raikes for approval.

3. At that point, Bob approves or disapproves the duplicate sample. Applause makes any necessary corrections at its overseas manufacturers.

Attractively displayed is Max, *from the 1986 2nd Edition of Raikes Bears by Applause.* Courtesy of Applause, Inc.

The wood carvers in the Philippines use many carving tools for the intricate work on the faces of the Raikes Bears. Courtesy of Applause, Inc.

A "Certificate of Authenticity" is enclosed in the collector's box with each limited edition Raikes Bear manufactured by Applause. Courtesy of Robert and Carol Raikes.

A carver hand-carves the face of the Raikes Bear design produced for Applause. The Filipinos take great pride in their work as Applause sets high quality control on the Raikes products. Note how the craftsman works on three faces at once. Courtesy of Applause, Inc.

This machine flap sands the carved wooden parts of the Raikes products. Courtesy of Applause, Inc.

The carved wooden pieces for the Raikes animals are placed on racks to dry. Courtesy of Applause, Inc.

An elf bear receives the final inspection before he is packaged and ready to be shipped to America. Courtesy of Applause, Inc.

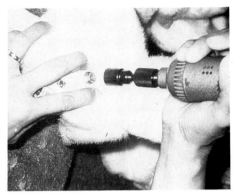

The limbs of the Raikes animals are securely bolted together with an electric wrench. Courtesy of Applause, Inc.

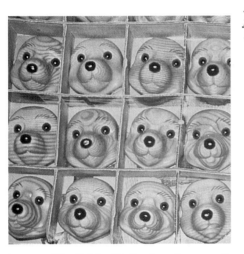

A group of the finished Raikes bear faces await assemblage. Courtesy of Applause, Inc.

Robert Raikes Creations by Applause
First Edition, Autumn 1985. Limited edition of 7500 of each design.
"From the hands of the artisan into your heart"
"*A truly collectible series of fully jointed bears with finely carved wooden faces and paws of select cypress. Each Raikes Original is carefully detailed. Imbued with a distinct personality that is as unique as the intricately detailed clothing each wears.*

"*Individually signed and numbered, these Robert Raikes limited edition Originals come boxed with their own certificate of authenticity, ownership registration card and hang tag.*

"*It's easy to see why collectors have already expressed real interest in these fine pieces and why Raikes Originals are destined to become collector classics.*
"The special creation of a special artist"
"*Born in the visionary mind of artist and sculptor Robert Raikes, the design of each Raikes Bear takes shape in the sculptor's hand over countless hours.*

"*Attention to detail is the designer's forte. The wood used must have just the right color, grain and overall feel. The fur for each bear can be only the finest plush material. The result is a stunning work of art.*

"*Applause is proud to offer you the opportunity to acquire a very special and most distinctive limited edition bear. "A Robert Raikes Original." (Raikes Collector Brochure, 1985.)*

(Left) Rebecca. *First Edition, Autumn 1985. Raikes Bear by Applause. 22in (56cm) tall; dark brown acrylic fur; carved wooden face and foot pads; inset plastic eyes; jointed arms and legs; swivel head; signed and numbered on foot; limited edition of 7500; style number 5447. "Wearing a two-piece dress with pinafore and satin ribbons. Rebecca is a very ladylike bear. She loves to be a trendsetter." (Raikes Collector Brochure, 1985.)*

(Right) Sebastian. *First Edition, Autumn 1985. Raikes Bear by Applause. 22in (56cm) tall; dark brown acrylic fur; carved wooden face and foot pads; inset plastic eyes; jointed arms and legs; swivel head; signed and numbered on foot; limited edition of 7500; style number 5445. "Peering at the world through wire spectacles, Sebastian wears a handsome plaid vest, velveteen bow tie and thinks of himself as dignified." (Raikes Collector Brochure, 1985.)* Courtesy of Robert and Carol Raikes.

(Left) Bently. *First Edition, Autumn 1985. Raikes Bear by Applause. 14in (36cm) tall; charcoal-colored acrylic fur; carved wooden face and foot pads; inset plastic eyes; jointed arms and legs; swivel head; signed and numbered on foot; limited edition of 7500; style number 5448. "He's quite a proper fellow, Bently. His tweed vest with a pocket has a timeless quality and his outfit is topped off with a velveteen bow tie." (Raikes Collector Brochure, 1985.)*

(Center) Chelsea. *First Edition, Autumn 1985. Raikes Bear by Applause. 14in (36cm) tall; brown acrylic fur; carved wooden face and foot pads; inset plastic eyes; jointed arms and legs; swivel head; signed and numbered on foot; limited edition of 7500; style number 5451. "Dressed in an adorable rust and blue print dress with satin ribbons, she's everyone's little sweetheart." (Raikes Collector Brochure, 1985.)*

(Right) Eric. *First Edition, Autumn 1985. Raikes Bear by Applause. 14in (36cm) tall; dark brown acrylic fur; carved wooden face and foot pads; inset plastic eyes; jointed arms and legs; swivel head; signed and numbered on foot; limited edition of 7500; style number 5449. "Outfitted with a knitted sweater, hat and scarf (with 'Raikes Bears' knitted right into it), Eric's one true love is skiing." (Raikes Collector Brochure, 1985.)* Courtesy of Robert and Carol Raikes.

(Left) Huckle Bear. *First Edition, August 1985. Raikes Bear by Applause. 22in (56cm) tall; gray acrylic fur; carved wooden face and foot pads; inset plastic eyes; jointed arms and legs; swivel head; signed and numbered on foot; limited edition of 7500; style number 5446.* "The farmer, Huckle Bear wears overalls with a real pocket that are perfect in every detail. He reads Mark Twain *in his spare time."* (Raikes Collector Brochure, 1985.) *Seated to the right of* Huckle Bear *is* Sherwood. *Courtesy of Robert and Carol Raikes.*

Jamie. *Autumn 1985. Raikes Bears by Applause. 10in (25cm) tall; (Left) gray acrylic fur; (Right) brown acrylic fur; carved wooden face and foot pads; inset plastic eyes; jointed arms and legs; swivel head; style number 5453.*

Unnumbered series. Jamie *was not manufactured with Robert Raikes' signature on the foot. The artist personally autographed these bears for the Woodmans at a teddy bear event.* Courtesy of Robert and Pat Woodman. Photograph by Robert Woodman.

Sherwood. *Autumn 1985. Raikes Bear by Applause. 13in (33cm) tall; (Left) dark brown acrylic fur; (Right) light brown acrylic fur; carved wooden face and foot pads; inset plastic eyes; jointed arms and legs; swivel head; style number 5452.*

Unnumbered series. Sherwood *was not manufactured with Robert Raikes' signature on the foot. The artist personally autographed these bears for the Woodmans at a teddy bear event.* Courtesy of Robert and Pat Woodman. Photograph by Robert Woodman.

Robert Raikes Creations by Applause
Second Edition, Spring 1986. Limited edition of 15,000 of each design.

"For those who cherish America's heritage, Applause presents the second collection of Raikes Bears."

"The Raikes Originals are carefully detailed and sculpted to portray the life and style of the 1890s. This truly collectible series of fully-jointed bears features all new finely carved faces and detailed paw pads of light stained cypress.

"Each bear from this limited edition series is individually signed, numbered and comes boxed with its own certificate of authenticity and an ownership registration card.

"This edition of Raikes Originals expands the Raikes Bears family to thirteen. These bears are destined to become collector classics, like their older cousins.

"Very special creations from a very special artist." (Raikes Collector Brochure, 1986.) Note: A special edition of the second series of Raikes Bears was produced by Applause for the United Kingdom. Marked "UK Limited Edition," it appears there were 100 each of Max, Kitty *and* Arnold *and 230 each of* Benjamin, Christopher *and* Penelope.

4. In the meantime, Applause starts working with the Art Department on a look for the Collector Box, Official Certificate of Authenticity, the Ownership Registration Card and the Raikes Collectors Brochure. The brochure is colorfully illustrated with valuable information regarding the artist and the animals. (Noted in the illustration captions are the products that include the Raikes Collectors Brochure.)

5. The artwork is sent to Bob for approval.

6. An identification hang-tag is attached to each animal's arm. In addition, the company's production label is sewn into the back seam.

7. The limited editions are hand-numbered on the foot and the majority of all products display the signature of Robert Raikes.

8. The product is produced.

9. The wood Applause uses for the Raikes bears is cypress, maple or white wood.

10. Robert Raikes approves all the names of the bears, but some of them have a cute history. For instance, Emily, Jenny and Jason were named after Robert Raikes' children.

So, at Applause, even a fantasy bear like a Raikes bear has a logical step-by-step birthing process prior to becoming a child's toy or a collector's treasure.

(Left) Kitty. *Second Edition, Spring 1986. Raikes Bear by Applause. 24in (61cm) tall; brown acrylic fur; carved wooden face and foot pads; inset plastic eyes; jointed arms and legs; swivel head; signed and numbered on foot; limited edition of 15,000; style number 5458. "This high-stepping gal will steal your heart in her old-fashioned pink lace blouse and full moiré fabric Can-Can skirt." (Raikes Collector Brochure, 1986.)*

(Right) Max. *Second Edition, Spring 1986. Raikes Bear by Applause. 24in (61cm) tall; charcoal-colored acrylic fur; carved wooden face and foot pads; inset plastic eyes; jointed arms and legs; swivel head; signed and numbered on foot; limited edition of 15,000; style number 5460. "Better watch your cards. Max is a real ole-time card dealer sporting the traditional visor, black corduroy vest and garter." (Raikes Collector Brochure, 1986.)* Courtesy of Robert and Carol Raikes.

Arnold. *Second Edition, Spring 1986. Raikes Bear by Applause. 24in (61cm) tall; light gray acrylic fur; carved wooden face and foot pads; inset plastic eyes; jointed arms and legs; swivel head; signed and numbered on foot; limited edition of 15,000; style number 5459. "Arnold is ready to hit the greens in his dapper knickers, argyle sweater and velveteen tie, all topped off with a matching Scottish cap." (Raikes Collector Brochure, 1986.)* Courtesy of Shirley Tish.

(Left) Christopher. *Second Edition, Spring 1986. Raikes Bear by Applause. 16in (41cm) tall; light brown acrylic fur; carved wooden face and foot pads; inset plastic eyes; jointed arms and legs; swivel head; signed and numbered on foot; limited edition of 15,000; style number 5455. "Off to the shore for a Sunday outing, Christopher's all decked out in a sailor's suit of red, white and blue complete with ribboned cap." (Raikes Collector Brochure, 1986.)*

(Right) Penelope. *Second Edition, Spring 1986. Raikes Bear by Applause. 16in (41cm) tall; beige acrylic fur; carved wooden face and foot pads; inset plastic eyes; jointed arms and legs; swivel head; signed and numbered on foot; limited edition of 15,000; style number 5457. "She's the life of the party and picture perfect in her pink party dress with lace detail and bow to match." (Raikes Collector Brochure, 1986.)* Courtesy of Robert and Carol Raikes.

Tyrone. *Second Edition, Spring 1986. Raikes Bear by Applause. 36in (91cm) tall; brown acrylic fur; carved wooden face and foot pads; inset plastic eyes; jointed arms and legs; stationary head; signed and numbered on foot; limited edition of 5000; style number 5461.* "All turned out in his black velvet and satin trimmed tux with pearl buttoned shirt. Tyrone will be the hit of the affair." (Raikes Collector Brochure, 1986.) Courtesy of Applause, Inc.

Benjamin. *Second Edition, Spring 1986. Raikes Bear by Applause. 16in (41cm) tall; dark brown acrylic fur; carved wooden face and foot pads; inset plastic eyes; jointed arms and legs; swivel head; signed and numbered on foot; limited edition of 15,000; style number 5456.* "Ready for bed. Benjamin will sleep warm and toasty in his soft blue flannel back-flapped jammies and matching stocking cap." *(Raikes Collector Brochure, 1986.)* Courtesy of Robert and Pat Woodman. Photograph by Robert Woodman.

Allison and Gregory, the Wedding Couple. *Summer 1986. Raikes Bears by Applause. 16in (41cm) tall; white acrylic fur; carved wooden face and foot pads; inset plastic eyes; jointed arms and legs; swivel head; signed and numbered on foot; limited edition numbered to 15,000 pairs; only 10,000 sets made; Allison— style number 5462. Dressed in bridal gown and veil. Gregory—style number 5462. Dressed in black velvet tuxedo, top hat, bow tie and white satin vest.*

Sold only as a pair in one collector box. One certificate per pair. Courtesy of Applause, Inc.

Robert Raikes Creations by Applause
Third Edition, Autumn 1986. Limited edition of 15,000 of each design.

Applause Presents the
"Glamour Bears of the 1920s"

"From Lindberg's flight across the Atlantic, to the glamorous stars of the silver screen, new found independence, jubilant flappers with a zest for life, typify the events of the 'Roaring 20s.'

"And now, Robert Raikes, the recognized artisan and sculptor, has masterfully captured in wood and plush as only he can, the personalities, characteristics and gaiety of the 20s era. Applause is proud to present this exclusive third edition of Robert Raikes Originals.

"Like all of Robert Raikes previous creations, these bears are fully-jointed and impeccably detailed, down to the embroidered 'Raikes Bears' name found on their clothing. This joyful series features new plush colors, and finely carved expressive faces and detailed paw pads all of lightly stained cypress.

"Individually signed and numbered, these limited editions of 15,000 each, come collector boxed with their own certificate of authenticity and ownership registration card." (Raikes Collector Brochure, 1986.)

Left) Lindy. *Third Edition, Autumn 1986. Raikes Bear by Applause. 24in (61cm) tall; brown acrylic fur; carved wooden face and foot pads; inset plastic eyes; jointed arms and legs; swivel head; signed and numbered on foot; limited edition of 15,000; style number 5463. "Ready for a tough flight across the Atlantic, Lindy's our leading man in his flight jacket, pilot's cap with goggles and World War I flying ace scarf." (Raikes Collector Brochure, 1986.)*

(Center) Daisy. *Third Edition, Autumn 1986. Raikes Bear by Applause. 16in (41cm) tall; variegated gray and black acrylic fur; carved wooden face and foot pads; inset plastic eyes; jointed arms and legs; swivel head; signed and numbered on foot; limited edition of* 15,000; style number 5468. "Daisy's right out of F. Scott Fitzgerald's *Great Gatsby. A member of the 'smart set,' she's stylishly dressed in a gray pleated skirt, sweater and pink felt cloche." (Raikes Collector Brochure, 1986.)*

(Right) Reginald. *Third Edition, Autumn 1986. Raikes Bear by Applause. 16in (41cm) tall; variegated gray and black acrylic fur; carved wooden face and foot pads; inset plastic eyes; jointed arms and legs; swivel head; signed and numbered on foot; limited edition of 15,000; style number 5467. "'Twenty-three skidoo!' In his felt beanie covered with popular slang buttons, argyle sweater, bow tie and class pennant our collegiate hero is ready to impress any girl he meets." (Raikes Collector Brochure, 1986.)* Courtesy of Applause, Inc.

(Left) Cecil. *Third Edition, Autumn 1986. Raikes Bear by Applause. 16in (41cm) tall; dark brown acrylic fur; carved wooden face and foot pads; inset plastic eyes; jointed arms and legs; swivel head; signed and numbered on foot; limited edition of 15,000; style number 5466. "Cecil's expression lets you know he's ready to shout 'Cut' but he's dressed for 'Action', complete with his director's megaphone, velvety red beret, monocle, satin ascot and khaki-colored safari jacket." (Raikes Collector Brochure, 1986.)*

(Center) Maude. *Third Edition, Autumn 1986. Raikes Bear by Applause. 24in (61cm) tall; white acrylic fur; carved wooden face and foot pads; inset plastic eyes; jointed arms and legs; swivel head; signed and numbered on foot; limited edition of 15,000; style number 5464. "Maude has everything it takes to be a 'silent-movie' star. From her roaring '20s flapper dress in pink and aqua pastels with black satin trim to her long strands of pearls and perky felt cloche." (Raikes Collector Brochure, 1986.)*

(Right) Zelda. *Third Edition, Autumn 1986. Raikes Bear by Applause. 16in (41cm) tall; white acrylic fur; carved wooden face and foot pads; inset plastic eyes; jointed arms and legs; swivel head; signed and numbered on foot; limited edition of 15,000; style number 5465. "Zelda's ready to cut a rug in her black fringed frock and sequined headband. Her little pout tells you she's one bear who's not happy unless she's doing The Charleston." (Raikes Collector Brochure, 1986.)* Courtesy of Applause, Inc.

Calvin *and* Rebecca. *Rabbits. Spring 1987. Raikes Rabbits by Applause. 18in (46cm) tall; carved wooden head and paws (jointed at ankles); painted eyes; unjointed cloth body.* Calvin—*style number 20137. Dressed in tweed pants and striped shirt.* Rebecca—*style number 20136. Dressed in floral dress with pinafore carrying a basket.*

First edition of rabbits. Unnumbered series. At this writing, 5000 of each have been produced. Calvin *and* Rebecca *were not manufactured with Robert Raikes' signature on the foot. Courtesy of Robert and Carol Raikes.*

Robert Raikes Creations by Applause
Fourth Edition, Spring 1987. Limited edition of 7500 of each design.

**Applause Presents the
"Americana Collection"**

Miss Melony. *"Americana Collection." Fourth Edition, Spring 1987. Raikes Bear by Applause. 24in (61cm) tall; brown acrylic fur; carved wooden face and paw pads; inset plastic eyes; jointed arms and legs; swivel head; signed and numbered on foot; limited edition of 7500; style number 17005. Dressed as a Southern Belle in a white and blue floral dress, white hat and blue tulle parasol. Courtesy of Robert and Pat Woodman. Photograph by Robert Woodman.*

Sara Anne. *"Americana Collection." Fourth Edition, Spring 1987. Raikes Bear by Applause. 16in (41cm) tall; cream-colored acrylic fur; carved wooden face and foot pads; inset plastic eyes; jointed arms and legs; swivel head; signed and numbered on foot; limited edition of 7500; style number 17002. Dressed in pink and white floral dress and hat. Courtesy of Robert and Pat Woodman. Photograph by Robert Woodman.*

Margaret. *"Americana Collection." Fourth Edition, Spring 1987. Raikes Bear by Applause. 16in (41cm) tall; white acrylic fur; carved wooden face and foot pads; inset plastic eyes; jointed arms and legs; swivel head; signed and numbered on foot; limited edition of 7500; style number 17004. Dressed in a nurse's uniform. Courtesy of Robert and Carol Raikes.*

Casey. *"Americana Collection." Fourth Edition, Spring 1987. Raikes Bear by Applause. 16in (41cm) tall; cream-colored acrylic fur; carved wooden face and foot pads; inset plastic eyes; jointed arms and legs; swivel head; signed and numbered on foot; limited edition of 7500; style number 17003. Dressed as a baseball player complete with baseball glove. Courtesy of Robert and Carol Raikes.*

Andrew *and* Jill. *Spring 1988. Raikes rabbits by Applause. 23in (58cm) tall (including ears); dark brown acrylic fur; carved wooden face; velveteen foot pads and inner ears; painted eyes; unjointed arms and legs; stationary head; signed and numbered on foot; limited edition of 5000 each. (Left) Andrew—style number 20267. Dressed in blue and white striped vest with pink satin tie. (Right) Jill—style number 20266. Dressed in white, pink and blue floral dress.*
Second series of Raikes Rabbits. Courtesy of Robert and Carol Raikes.

Robert Raikes Creations by Applause
Beavers. Spring 1988. Limited edition of 5000 of each design.

Applause Presents the "Timber Creek Collection"

"Journey with us deep into the forest, far from the world of man. Peering through the trees, into a tiny clearing next to a gentle stream, we happen upon a bustling community of a different sort, The Beavers of Timber Creek.

"The Timber Creek Collection is the latest creation of the masterful artisan and sculptor, Robert Raikes, the creator of bears and rabbits. Through keen observation of his neighbors in the wilderness near his Mt. Shasta home, Robert Raikes captured the true nature of these unique and fascinating creatures, and interpreted them in his own inimitable style.

"The Beavers of Timber Creek are by nature busy little animals, yet we find them at

a rare moment of leisure. Beaming at us with sweet, expressive faces, dressed in their best, each is a joyful reminder of the satisfaction which comes from a job well done.

"In limited editions of 5000, these new designs carry on the Raikes tradition of exquisitely detailed collectibles, finely crafted in delicately carved cypress and luxurious plush. And, of course, every piece in the collection is numbered and bears the signature of its creator.

"The Timber Creek Collection—an irresistible addition to the habitat you call home." (Raikes Collector Brochure, 1988.)
Sam and Lucy. "Timber Creek Collection." *Spring 1988. Raikes Beavers by Applause. 14in (36cm) tall; dark brown acrylic fur; dark brown velveteen tail; carved wooden face, feet and paws; inset plastic eyes; jointed arms and legs; stationary head; signed and numbered on foot; limited edition of 5000 each. (Left)*

Sam—*style number 17012. "Sam is wearing a sailor top, the same exquisite detailing as Lucy's. He also sports a white knit beret, which adds that special accent." (Raikes Collector Brochure, 1988.) (Right)* Lucy—*style number 17011. "Lucy is dressed for the country in a white sailor top beautifully detailed with navy blue ribbon edging and a red tie and a pleated skirt. Her big blue bow adds the finishing touch for a day in the country." (Raikes Collector Brochure, 1988.) Collector's tip. A percentage of Lucy's ties bore the name "Raikes Bears." Corrected ties read "Raikes Originals." Courtesy of Robert and Carol Raikes.*

Robert Raikes Creation by Applause
Fifth Edition, Spring 1988. Limited Edition of 7500 of each design.

Applause Presents the "Sweet Sunday Collection"

"No one can resist the sweetness and innocence of a little toddler. And these little ones come straight from the nursery and into your heart.

"Capturing the very essence of a toddler's personality, the Sweet Sunday Collection is our newest Limited Edition of Raikes Bears.

"These bundles of joy are all dressed up in their Sunday Best and are, of course, on their best behavior.

"Only Robert Raikes, the masterful artisan and sculptor, could capture the softness of youth in the beautiful blend of wood and plush. These fully-jointed collectible bears are exquisitely detailed. From the satin ribbons in their hair to the eyelet petticoats to the embroidered designer name on their clothing.

"This lovable new collection captures the sweet rosy-cheeked innocence that adorns these baby's faces and sets them apart from the elder members of the Raikes family. Their lasting appeal is enhanced by the finely-carved and lightly-stained faces and paw pads.

"Individually signed and numbered, each Limited Edition of 7500 bears comes with its own collector box, Certificate of Authenticity, ownership registration card and this 5th Edition Raikes Collector Brochure.

"If you were lucky enough to acquire any or all of the first four editions of Raikes Bears, you already know that their market value has increased many fold since their introduction." (Raikes Collector Brochure, 1988.)

(Left) Susie. *"Sweet Sunday Collection." Fifth Edition, Spring 1988. Raikes Bear by Applause. 16in (41cm) tall; light brown acrylic fur; carved wooden face and foot pads; inset plastic eyes; jointed arms and legs; swivel head; signed and numbered on foot; limited edition of 7500; style number 17008. "I look forward all week to Sunday. That's when I put on my pretty pantaloons and dress up in my pink and blue flowered dress. The special one with the matching bonnet." (Raikes Collector Brochure, 1988.)*

(Center) Sally. *"Sweet Sunday Collection." Fifth Edition, Spring 1988. Raikes Bear by Applause. 16in (41cm) tall; white acrylic fur; carved wooden face and foot pads; inset plastic eyes; jointed arms and legs; swivel head; signed and numbered on foot; limited edition*

of 7500; style number 17007. "I love when mom puts the pink satin bow in my hair. Nobody can resist my charms when I toddle out in my pink cotton dress with the dainty flower pattern and applique trim." (Raikes Collector Brochure, 1988.)

(Right) Timmy. *"Sweet Sunday Collection." Fifth Edition, Spring 1988. Raikes Bear by Applause. 16in (41cm) tall; dark brown acrylic fur; carved wooden face and foot pads; inset plastic eyes; jointed arms and legs; swivel head; signed and numbered on foot; limited edition of 7500; style number 17009. "Mom's always dressing me in 'her' favorite blue and white plaid playsuit with matching bow tie. At least the cotton weave feels light and comfortable to play around in." (Raikes Collector Brochure, 1988.)* Courtesy of Applause, Inc.

Terry. *Summer 1988. Raikes Bear by Applause. 12in (31cm) tall; available in brown or white acrylic fur; carved wooden face and foot pads; inset plastic eyes; jointed arms and legs; swivel head; signed on foot; style number 17010.*

Unnumbered series. At this writing, 15,000 have been produced. Robert Raikes personally autographed these bears for the Woodmans at a teddy bear event. The Terry bear was also made in "black" acrylic fur (Center) as the Robert Raikes Collector's Club bear. Upon becoming a member, you receive one black Terry bear. (For more information on the Robert Raikes Collector's Club and the club bear, please refer to Chapter Two—The Robert Raikes Collector's Club and Disney Conventions.) Courtesy of Robert and Pat Woodman. Photograph by Robert Woodman.

Robert Raikes Creations by Applause
Sixth Edition, Summer 1988. Limited edition of 10,000 of each design.

Applause Presents the "Home Sweet Home Collection"

"Hot apple pie, cool glasses of lemonade, and Sunday dinner are just a taste of the warm and loving feelings of the Raikes Bears' Home Sweet Home Collection. Peek out the front window and see Emily, Jenny and Jason. These three siblings are the newest addition to the Raikes family. Charmingly crafted by the masterful artisan and sculptor, Robert Raikes, this collection will truly take you on a walk down memory lane with recollections of playtime on the porch, long talks on the swing, and warm breezes through the trees. Each bear beautifully depicts a "down-home" feeling, and their adorable faces are sure to touch your heart and conjure up reflections of your childhood." (Raikes Collector Brochure, 1988.)

(Left) Jason. *"Home Sweet Home Collection."* *Sixth Edition, Summer 1988. Raikes Bear by Applause. 18in (46cm) tall; dark brown acrylic fur; carved wooden face and foot pads; inset plastic eyes; jointed arms and legs; swivel head; signed and numbered on foot; limited edition of 10,000; style number 17015.* "Bespectacled Jason is irresistible with his button nose and charming waistcoat. His endearing face will tug at your heart strings and evoke a timeless feeling of the pleasant memories of bygone days. All three siblings will make you smile and tempt you to open up your 'Home Sweet Home' to their entire family." *(Raikes Collector Brochure, 1988.)*

(Right) Jenny. *"Home Sweet Home Collection." Sixth Edition, Summer 1988. Raikes Bear by Applause. 18in (46cm) tall; brown acrylic fur; carved wooden face and foot pads; inset plastic eyes; jointed arms and legs; swivel head; signed and numbered on foot; limited edition of 10,000; style number 17014.* "Jenny is a dainty little lady whose outfit is made of short heart print fabric edged with lace and accented with heart shaped buttons. Her petite night cap frames her adorable face with lace, reflecting the beautiful handcrafted design that has been demonstrated throughout all of Robert Raikes collections." *(Raikes Collector Brochure, 1988.)* Courtesy of Robert and Carol Raikes.

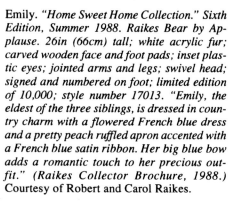

Emily. *"Home Sweet Home Collection." Sixth Edition, Summer 1988. Raikes Bear by Applause. 26in (66cm) tall; white acrylic fur; carved wooden face and foot pads; inset plastic eyes; jointed arms and legs; swivel head; signed and numbered on foot; limited edition of 10,000; style number 17013.* "Emily, the eldest of the three siblings, is dressed in country charm with a flowered French blue dress and a pretty peach ruffled apron accented with a French blue satin ribbon. Her big blue bow adds a romantic touch to her precious outfit." *(Raikes Collector Brochure, 1988.)* Courtesy of Robert and Carol Raikes.

Kevi. *Autumn 1988. Raikes Bear by Applause. 12in (31cm) tall; light brown acrylic fur; carved wooden face and foot pads; inset plastic eyes; unjointed arms and legs; stationary head; signed and numbered on foot; limited edition of 10,000; style number 17019.*

The concept for the Kevi bear came to Bob after he had met the internationally acclaimed singer and entertainer Kevin Roth. Bob was so impressed with the children's response to Kevin and his singing that Bob had the idea to make a bear with a tape recording ("Unbearable Bears") of Kevin's singing accompanying the bear. Courtesy of Robert and Pat Woodman. Photograph by Robert Woodman.

Left) Mrs. Claus. *Christmas 1988. Raikes Bear by Applause. 17in (43cm) tall; white acrylic fur; carved wooden face and foot pads; inset plastic eyes; jointed arms and legs; swivel head; signed and numbered on foot; limited edition of 7500; style number 21391. Dressed in wine-colored velvet dress with beige lace apron.*

(Right) Santa Claus. *Christmas 1988. Raikes Bear by Applause. 17in (43cm) tall; white acrylic fur; carved wooden face, beard and foot pads; inset plastic eyes; jointed arms and legs; swivel head; signed and numbered on foot; limited edition of 7500; style number 21390. Dressed in wine-colored velvet Santa Claus outfit.*

First Christmas edition. Courtesy of Robert and Carol Raikes.

(Left) Brett. *1989. Raikes Rabbit by Applause. 11in (28cm) tall; brown acrylic fur; light brown velveteen foot pads and inner ears; inset "blue" plastic eyes; unjointed arms and legs; stationary head; whiskers; signed on foot; style number 2041. Dressed in white pants and pink shirt.*

(Center Left) Ashley. *1989. Raikes Rabbit by Applause. 11in (28cm) tall; brown acrylic fur; light brown velveteen foot pads and inner ears; inset "blue" plastic eyes; unjointed arms and legs; stationary head; whiskers; signed on foot; style number 20400. Dressed in white and pink sun dress.*

Brett *and* Ashley *are an unnumbered series. At this writing, 15,000 of each have been produced. Note this is the first time Applause had used blue eyes on Robert Raikes animals.* (Center Right) Mr. Nickleby. *Easter 1989. Raikes Rabbit by Applause. 16in (41cm) tall (ears not included); brown acrylic fur; light brown velveteen foot pads (sculptured) and inner ears; inset plastic eyes; jointed arms and legs; swivel head; whiskers; signed and numbered on foot; limited edition of 7500; style number 20399. Dressed in pink and white print dress and white hat.*

(Right) Mrs. Nickleby. *Easter 1989. Raikes Rabbit by Applause. 16in (41cm) tall; brown acrylic fur; light brown velveteen foot pads (sculptured) and inner ears; inset plastic eyes; jointed arms and legs; swivel head; whiskers; signed and numbered on foot; limited edition of 7500; style number 20398. Dressed in white shirt and slacks with a corduroy vest.*

Third edition of Raikes Rabbits. Courtesy of Applause, Inc.

Robert Raikes Creations by
The Good Company

Seventh Edition, Spring 1989. Limited edition of 10,000 of each design.

The Good Company Presents the
"Saturday Matinee Collection"

"Close your eyes and journey back to a simpler time. A time of jukeboxes, Saturday afternoon movies, bobby sox, and youthful innocence.

"It's the 50s and Robert Raikes, the masterful artisan and sculptor, has once again captured the spirit of the decade with his seventh edition, the Saturday Matinee Collection.

"Exquisitely detailed, these bears relive the playfulness of the 50s in an adorable blend of wood and plush, adorned by the costumes of their silver screen heroes.

"In keeping with Raikes' highest standards of excellence, these fully-jointed, finely crafted collectibles are in limited editions of 10,000 each. They come with their own Collector Box, Certificate of Authenticity and Ownership Registration Card. And, of course, each and every piece is numbered and bears the signature of its creator.

"Close your eyes...You can almost taste the popcorn, hear the thunder of hoofbeats and feel the $.35 ticket stub in your hand...Now open them. It's the Raikes Saturday Matinee Collection." (Raikes Collector Brochure, 1989.)

(Left) Lionel. *"Saturday Matinee Collection." Seventh Edition, Spring 1989. Raikes Bear by The Good Company. 24in (61cm) tall; brown acrylic fur; carved wooden face and foot pads; inset plastic eyes; jointed arms and legs; swivel head; signed and numbered on foot; limited edition of 10,000; style number 660281. "Lionel is the embodiment of Casey Jones himself in his engineer striped blue overalls and cap. Like any tyke following in the footsteps of his hero, he realizes the importance of accuracy and polishes off his look with a red bandana before 'headin' to the matinee." (Raikes Collector Brochure, 1989.)*

(Center) Bonnie. *"Saturday Matinee Collection." Seventh Edition, Spring 1989. Raikes Bear by The Good Company. 18in (46cm) tall; medium beige acrylic fur; carved wooden face and foot pads; inset plastic eyes; jointed arms and legs; swivel head; signed and numbered on foot; limited edition of 10,000; style number 660280. "Bonnie is the square dancer's favorite as she complements her hero, Jesse. In a darlin' blue denim skirt with white eyelet trim, red and white gingham blouse, and white cotton petticoat, she's ready for a Saturday afternoon with her best boy. She even has a matching 'cowgirl' hat!" (Raikes Collector Brochure, 1989.)*

(Right) Jesse. *"Saturday Matinee Collection." Seventh Edition, Spring 1989. Raikes Bear by The Good Company. 18in (46cm) tall; light beige acrylic fur; carved wooden face and foot pads; inset plastic eyes; jointed arms and legs; swivel head; signed and numbered on foot; limited edition of 10,000; style number 660279. "Yee-Haw! Jesse is rootin'-tootin' ready for his favorite Matinee in his blue denim jeans and red flannel shirt. His little white vest with Sheriff's star, cowboy hat, and red bandana neckerchief could even bring a smile to anyone's face!" (Raikes Collector Brochure, 1989.)*

It appears the style numbers on the bears do not coincide with the Raikes Collector Brochure. The style numbers on the bear are as follows: Jesse #17021, Bonnie #17022, Lionel #17023. In addition, the size of Lionel in the Raikes Collector Brochure is 24in (61cm) and the bear measures 18in (46cm). Courtesy of The Good Company.

(Left) Lionel. "Saturday Matinee Collection." Seventh Edition, Spring 1989. Raikes Bear by The Good Company. 18in (46cm) tall.

(Right) Lionel (Artist Proof). "Saturday Matinee Collection." Seventh Edition, Spring 1989. Raikes Bear by The Good Company. 18in (46cm) tall.

Note the distinctive difference between the two bears. The Artist Proof's hat is sewn on the left, the "Raikes Bears" stitching (plural). "AP" precedes number on foot, production tag sewn on back reads "Product of Taiwan ROC," not "Made in the Philippines." Applause "Artist Proofs" are models given to Production to create the Originals. There are generally 350 of each model made. They are not for sale but sometimes slip through into the retailers' market. They are a rarity and in some cases more valuable than the Originals themselves. An interesting article about Lionel was published in the Fall 1989 issue of Bearrister Bugle (now Raikes Review):

"Out of the 10,000-piece production run, a small number of rare Lionels which are distinctively different from the majority, were released to the general public.

"In February of 1989, Applause/Good introduced the 'Saturday Matinee Collection,' the seventh edition of Raikes Bears by that company. This set, made up of Jesse the Cowboy, Bonnie the Cowgirl, and Lionel the Train Engineer, had a limited production run of 10,000 pieces each.

"According to Joe Dumbacher, a production manager at Applause/Good in Woodland Hills, California, 390 of the Lionels produced were made in Taiwan rather than the Philippines, where the rest of the 'Saturday Matinee Collection' pieces were manufactured.

"These 'Taiwan Lionels' are distinguished from the majority as follows: The hat is perched on his left rather than on his right; the number on the foot is preceded by "AP"; the production tag is located at his upper back rather than near the tail and reads 'Product of Taiwan, ROC' rather than 'Made in the Philippines;' and the stitching on his overalls reads 'Raikes Bears'(plural); (The debate as to whether 'Raikes Bear,' which is stitched on all other Saturday Matinee pieces, was a deviation from the registered trademark and thus itself a production error is another story.)

"Why 'AP,' for Artist Proof, was stamped on these 390 Lionels is not clear. A true Artist Proof Lionel, noted by AP on the foot with no number, was auctioned off by Robert Raikes at the October 1988 Briston, Connecticut bear show. Happily, that true artist proof was purchased by a fellow Raikes-collecting couple.

"One more point, Taiwan Lionels are not simply Lionels 1 through 390. For example, number 320/10,000 is not a Taiwan piece. Thus, these 'AP' bears are not consecutively numbered." Information courtesy of Michael L. Swindler, editor of Raikes Review. Photograph courtesy of Robert and Pat Woodman.

Annie. "Mother's Day Collection." 1989. Raikes Bear by The Good Company. 16in (41cm) tall; white acrylic fur; carved wooden face and foot pads; inset plastic eyes; jointed arms and legs; swivel head; signed and numbered on foot; limited edition of 7500; style number 660283. Dressed in pink and white dress. Courtesy of The Good Company.

Cookie. *Spring 1989. Raikes Bears by The Good Company. 12in (31cm) tall; available in brown or gray acrylic fur; carved wooden face and foot pads; inset plastic eyes; jointed arms and legs; swivel head; signed on foot.*

Unnumbered series. At this writing, 30,000 have been produced. Robert Raikes personally autographed these bears for the Woodmans at a teddy bear event. Courtesy of Robert and Pat Woodman. Photograph by Robert Woodman.

(Left) Juliet. *Spring 1989. Raikes doll by The Good Company. 14in (36cm) tall; carved wooden head and arms; painted blue eyes; unjointed cloth body; signed and numbered on back; edition of 7500; style number 660285. Dressed in christening outfit.*

Comes in a basket. First edition of Raikes dolls. This design was reproduced from Robert Raikes original one-of-a-kind baby doll.
(Right) Molly. *Spring 1989. Raikes doll by The Good Company. 16in (41cm) tall; carved wooden head, arms and legs; painted brown eyes; unjointed cloth body; black hair; signed on back of doll in black ink "A Robert Raikes;" comes with stand; signed and numbered on stand; limited edition of 7500; style number 660284. Dressed in pink gingham dress.*

Molly *and* Juliet *are the first edition of Raikes dolls. The design for* Molly *was taken from Robert Raikes original* Molly *doll.* Courtesy of The Good Company.

(Left) Marion Hedgehog. *"Sherwood Forest Collection."* Spring 1989. Raikes Hedgehog by The Good Company. 20in (51cm) tall; variegated dark brown acrylic fur; carved wooden face, paws and feet; inset plastic eyes; jointed arms and legs; swivel head; signed and numbered on foot; limited edition of 7500; style number 660332. Dressed in gold, beige and pink satin dress and burgundy and pink cape. *(Right)* Robin Raccoon. *"Sherwood Forest Collection."* Spring 1989. Raikes Raccoon by The Good Company. 16in (41cm) tall; a variegated brown acrylic fur; carved wooden face, paws and feet; inset plastic eyes; jointed arms and legs; swivel head; signed and numbered on foot; limited edition of 7500; style number 660331. Dressed as Robin Hood. Courtesy of The Good Company.

Liza. *Summer 1989. Raikes Bear by The Good Company. 13in (33cm) tall; white acrylic fur; carved wooden face and foot pads; inset plastic blue eyes; unjointed arms and legs; stationary head; signed and numbered on foot; edition of 10,000; style number 660376. Dressed in pink and white dress.*

A tape recording ("The Secret Journey Bear Lovin") of world famous singer and entertainer Kevin Roth accompanies the bear. Note this is the first Robert Raikes Bear produced by Applause and The Good Company with blue eyes. Courtesy of The Good Company.

(Top Row) Santa. *(Prototype.) Christmas 1989. Raikes Bear by The Good Company. 14in (36cm) tall; white acrylic fur; carved wooden face, beard and foot pads; inset plastic eyes; jointed arms and legs; swivel head; signed and numbered on foot; limited edition of 7500; style number 660334. Dressed in Santa Claus outfit.*

Second edition of a Santa Claus. The sack is for display purposes only.
(Bottom Row) Elves. *(Prototype.) Christmas 1989. Raikes Bears by The Good Company. 12in (31cm) tall; white acrylic fur; carved wooden face and foot pads; inset plastic eyes; jointed arms and legs; swivel head; signed on foot; unnumbered series. At this writing, 20,000 have been produced; style number 660335. Available in red or green corduroy elf outfits.*

The style of the outfits appears to vary slightly within edition. Courtesy of The Good Company.

Robert Raikes Creations by Applause
The Three Bears. Autumn 1989. Limited edition of 7500.

"They're No Fairy Tale"

"Once upon a time, a brilliant sculptor named Robert Raikes, introduced the world to a remarkable band of bears. In a few short years, the Raikes Bears have become known and loved throughout the world and are now one of the most prized collectibles in existence.

"The Good Company is proud to be associated with Mr. Raikes and is very privileged to announce that a whole new Bear family is about to emerge from the woods. Meet The Three Bears: Papa, Mama and Baby.

"You'll lose your heart the first time you see these captivating creatures. Each one is a fine example of the outstanding quality and incredible attention to detail that have always been the hallmark of Raikes Bears.

"This furry family is so lifelike that you'll swear they're whispering together every time you turn your back. Probably wondering if you're related to that little girl who caused them so much trouble.

"You'd better reserve a set right away because these are destined to be rare bears indeed. Only 7500 signed and numbered sets will be produced so it would be easy to miss out.

"Of course, the good news is, that even when you're just eating porridge, relaxing in an easy chair or snuggled safely in bed, these Raikes Bears will be increasing in value. Year after year.

"That's no fairy tale. That's for real. Because, like a good fairy tale, a Raikes Bear only gets better as time goes by." (**Teddy Bear & friends ®**, *December 1989.*)

The Three Bears. Autumn 1989. Raikes Bears by The Good Company.
(Left) Father Bear. *12in (31cm) tall; short dark brown acrylic fur; carved wooden face, paws and feet; inset plastic eyes; unjointed arms and legs; stationary head; signed and numbered on foot. Dressed in brown tweed trousers, cream-colored shirt with bow tie.*
(Center) Baby Bear. *7½in (18cm) tall; short dark brown acrylic fur; carved wooden face, paws and feet; inset plastic eyes; unjointed arms and legs; stationary head; signed and numbered on foot.*

(Right) Mother Bear. *12in (31cm) tall; short light brown acrylic fur; carved wooden face, paws and feet; inset plastic eyes; unjointed arms and legs; stationary head; signed and numbered on foot. Dressed in brown skirt, cream-colored blouse, pink apron and cap.*

The Three Bears *are mounted on a wooden base. Style number for all three bears is 661434. A limited edition of 7500 sets. Courtesy of The Good Company.*

Robert Raikes Creations by The Good Company

Eighth Edition, Spring 1990. Limited edition of 7500 of each design.

"Summer Fun at Camp Grizzly..."

"Relive the nostalgic memories of your first summer camp—the tangy scent of pine trees, the clean mountain air, the warmth of a campfire and the crispy sweetness of roasted marshmallows.

"In this, his eighth edition, the masterful artisan and sculptor, Robert Raikes, has captured the fun, excitement and woes of a child's first camping expedition with the 'Camp Grizzly' trio of characters dressed in authentic camping gear.

"The Camp Grizzly Collection continues the Raikes tradition of collectibility with a theme that has special appeal to children and adults alike. Each of Robert Raikes' creations increases in value over the years and the Camp Grizzly Collection promises to be no exception. These fully-jointed, finely crafted collectibles are in limited editions of 7500 pieces each. They come with their own Collector Box, Certificate of Authenticity and Ownership Registration Card. And, of course, each and every piece is numbered, with the signature of its creator." (Raikes Collector Brochure, 1990.)

Jeremy. *"Camp Grizzly Collection." Eighth Edition, Autumn 1989. Raikes Bears by The Good Company.* 16in (41cm) tall; dark cinnamon-colored acrylic fur; carved wooden face and foot pads; inset plastic eyes; jointed arms and legs; swivel head; signed and numbered on foot; limited edition of 7500; style number 661432. *"Ruggedly attired in cap, vest, shorts, and orange scarf, Jeremy tugs at the heart. With his pouting expression, he reflects the trepidation that accompanies the unknown." (Raikes Collector Brochure, 1990.)* Courtesy of The Good Company.

Hillary. *"Camp Grizzly Collection." Eighth Edition, Autumn 1989. Raikes Bears by The Good Company.* 16in (41cm) tall; dark cinnamon-colored acrylic fur; carved wooden face and foot pads; inset plastic eyes; jointed arms and legs; swivel head; signed and numbered on foot; limited edition of 7500; style number 661431. *"With her cheerful face and bright orange windbreaker, Hillary portrays all the eagerness and exuberance of a young girl on her first adventure." (Raikes Collector Brochure, 1990.)* Courtesy of The Good Company.

Wendell. *"Camp Grizzly Collection." Eighth Edition, Autumn 1989. Raikes Bears by The Good Company.* 24in (61cm) tall; dark brown acrylic fur; carved wooden face and foot pads; inset plastic eyes; jointed arms and legs; swivel head; signed and numbered on foot; limited edition of 7500; style number 661430. *"Wendell is the Camp Master, inspiring memories of camp leaders who protected us from the perils of the great outdoors. From his Smokey the Bear hat to his backpack, suspenders, and whistle, Wendell is the spitting image of authority." (Raikes Collector Brochure, 1990.)* Courtesy of The Good Company.

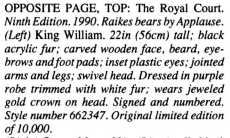

OPPOSITE PAGE, TOP: The Royal Court. *Ninth Edition. 1990. Raikes bears by Applause.* (Left) King William. *22in (56cm) tall; black acrylic fur; carved wooden face, beard, eyebrows and foot pads; inset plastic eyes; jointed arms and legs; swivel head. Dressed in purple robe trimmed with white fur; wears jeweled gold crown on head. Signed and numbered. Style number 662347. Original limited edition of 10,000.*

(Right) Queen Mary. *22in (56cm) tall; black acrylic fur; carved wooden face and foot pads; inset plastic eyes; jointed arms and legs; swivel head. Dressed in red and black dress trimmed in gold; wears jeweled gold crown on head.*

Signed and numbered. Style number 662348. Original limited edition of 10,000.

(Center) Court Jester. *14in (36cm); white acrylic fur; carved wooden face and foot pads; inset plastic eyes; jointed arms and legs; swivel head. Dressed in purple, yellow and mauve satin outfit and hat. Holds scepter with carved wooden face with jester hat. Signed and numbered. Style number 662349. Limited edition of 10,000. Sold as set. Note: Applause re-dressed 1500 of the King and Queen as* Diamond Jim Brady *and* Miss Ruby. *They were then released as a special limited edition.*
Courtesy Ed and Liz Oerding. Photograph by Ed Oerding.

Each limited edition of Raikes creations by Applause is hand-numbered (example: X2254/ 7500 is piece number 2254 out of 7500) and displays the signature of Robert Raikes. The unnumbered series just displays Robert Raikes' signature. With the exception of Jamie, Sherwood, Calvin *and* Rebecca, *their feet were blank (no signature or number).* Courtesy of Robert and Pat Woodman. Photograph by Robert Woodman.

Sophie. *Valentine Bear. Winter 1990. Raikes Bear by The Good Company. 12in (31cm) tall; white acrylic fur; carved wooden face and foot pads; inset plastic eyes; jointed arms and legs; swivel head; signed on foot; style number 661380. Wearing white ruffle with pink ribbon around neck; pink ribbon bow at ear.*

Note foot pads carved in the shape of a heart. Unnumbered series. Courtesy of The Good Company.

Best Friends Collection. Tenth Edition. 1991.
Raikes bears and animals by Applause.
(Left) Brian and Sport. Brian. 16in (41cm) tall;
brown acrylic fur; carved wooden face and foot
pads; inset plastic eyes; jointed arms and legs;
swivel head. Dressed in blue and white striped
jumper with a white cotton jersey. Signed and
numbered. Style number 38516. Sport. 4½in
(11cm) tall; beige acrylic fur; carved wooden
face; inset plastic eyes; unjointed legs; stationary head. Limited edition of 10,000.
(Right) Stacie and Fifi. Stacie. 16in (41cm) tall;
beige acrylic fur; carved wooden face and foot
pads; inset plastic eyes; jointed arms and legs;
swivel head. Dressed in blue and white gingham dress trimmed with floral print; lace rosette at ear. Signed and numbered. Style number 38517. Limited edition of 10,000. Fifi. 4½in
(11cm) tall; white acrylic fur; carved wooden
face; inset plastic blue eyes; unjointed legs;
stationary head. Limited edition of 10,000.
Courtesy Applause.

Minature Memories. Second Edition 1991.
(Left to right) Casey, Rebecca, Tyrone and
Annie. 1½in (4cm) tall. Including dome and
base 3in (8cm). It may take more than a year for
a Raikes miniature to be produced—but collectors the world over agree it's worth the wait!

Bob Raikes and Applause select the designs for the 2in (5cm) figurines and dome
figures. A skilled Taiwanese sculptor then follows Raikes' approved Applause Design Department renderings for final review. Any revi-
sions are made and when both Applause and
Bob Raikes are satisfied, silicone molds are
created. Resin is poured into the mold and
within 30 minutes hardens sufficiently to be
extracted, trimmed, polished and hand-painted.

Once again the piece goes through an
approval process with Applause and Bob Raikes.

Applause's Design Team completes the
packaging and sends the final art to Taiwan for
printing and manufacturing.

The end result is a Raikes miniature in a
glass dome. The figurines are not permanently
mounted on their wood base which provides a
"higher quality collectible" according to Applause.

Applause also manufactures musical
"snowdomes" which are not numbered or limited editions. Applause claims 10,000 each are
in circulation.

Some of these favorites are Eric ("Let it
Snow"), Susie, Timmy and Sally ("My Favorite
Things"), Tyrone and Kitty ("The Anniversary
Waltz"), Penelope ("The Sound of Music") and
Benjamin ("Brahms Lullaby").
Courtesy Robert and Pat Woodman. Photo-
graph by Bob Woodman.

Lindy, Jr. and Amelia. Eleventh Edition. 1991.
Raikes bears by Applause.

(Right) Lindy, Jr. 12in (31cm) tall; cream-
colored acrylic fur; carved wooden face and
foot pads; inset plastic eyes; jointed arms and
legs; swivel head. Dressed in brown bomber
jacket, cap and goggles. Signed and numbered.
Style number 38556. Limited edition of 10,000.
(Left) Amelia. 12in (31cm) tall; cream-colored
acrylic fur; carved wooden face and foot pads;
inset plastic eyes; jointed arms and legs; swivel
head. Dressed in pink bomber jacket with matching cap and goggles. Signed and numbered.
Style number 38557. Limited edition of 10,000.
Courtesy Robert and Pat Woodman. Photograph by Robert Woodman.

Santa Bear and Kathy Bear. *Christmas Edition. 1992. Raikes bears by Applause.* Santa Bear. *19in (48cm) tall; dual-colored gray acrylic fur; carved wooden face, moustache, beard, eyebrows and boots; inset plastic eyes; jointed arms and legs; swivel head. Dressed in traditional red and white Santa outfit. Signed and numbered. Style number 51488. Limited edition of 7500.*
Kathy Bear. *16in (41cm) tall; pale beige acrylic fur; carved wooden face and foot pads; inset plastic eyes; jointed arms and legs; swivel head. Dressed in a bright green dress trimmed in red with red ear muffs. Signed and numbered. Style number 51489. Limited edition of 7500. Courtesy Applause.*

Sidney and Charmaine. *Mother's Day Edition. 1992. Raikes cats by Applause. 12in (31cm) tall. (Left)* Charmaine. *White acrylic fur; carved wooden face and foot pads; inset green plastic eyes; jointed arms and legs; swivel head. Dressed in white with rose floral print dress; striped ruffle and bow on her head. Signed and numbered. Style number 38559. Limited edition of 7500.*
(Right) Sidney. *Dual-colored brown acrylic fur; carved wooden face and foot pads; inset green plastic eyes; jointed arms and legs; swivel head. Dressed in pink, white and green striped vest, white shirt and green bow tie. Signed and numbered. Style number 38558. Limited edition of 7500. Courtesy Applause.*

(Left) Diamond Jim Brady. *1992. Raikes bear by Applause. 21in (53cm) tall; black acrylic fur; carved wooden face, beard, eyebrows and foot pads; inset plastic eyes; jointed arms and legs; swivel head. Dressed in a gray vest, white dicky, black bow tie and gray slacks. Numbered and hand signed by Robert Raikes. Serial number 38586. Limited edition of 1500.*
(Right) Ruby the Dance Hall Girl. *1993. Raikes bear by Applause. 21in (53cm); black acrylic fur; carved wooden face and foot pads; inset*

plastic eyes; jointed arms and legs; swivel head. Dressed in black net blouse, red satin dress trimmed with sequins, red feather at ear and wearing red slippers. Hand-numbered and signed by Robert Raikes. Serial number 38587. Limited edition of 1500.

Applause is to be commended for its marketing acumen in turning what were originally part of the Fall 1990 Royal Court Collection, King William and Queen Mary, into a new,

limited edition set of Diamond Jim Brady and Ruby, the Dance Hall Girl.

All it took was a change in costume to metamorphosize this unwanted inventory into a vitally popular duo.

In this reincarnation, the paw pads of these fancy bears were refinished and renumbered. Raikes signed 3000 pieces, marking the first time an Applause Raikes piece arrived at a retail level already autographed by the artist. Courtesy Applause.

Bob and Carol. *Second Edition Wedding Set. 1992. Raikes bears by Applause. 7in (18cm) tall.*
(Left) Bob. *Black acrylic fur; carved wooden face and foot pads; inset plastic eyes; jointed arms and legs; swivel head. Dressed in black tuxedo, top hat, gray vest with black and white striped tie. Signed and numbered. Style number 38577. Limited edition of 7500 (sold as a set). Boxed with* one certificate. The certificate is designed to be filled out by a real Bride and Groom.
(Right) Carol. *White acrylic fur; carved wooden face and foot pads; inset plastic eyes; jointed arms and legs; swivel head. Dressed in traditional white satin and lace wedding dress and veil. Signed and numbered. Style number 38577.*
Courtesy Applause.

Alec and Allison."The Picnic Pair." 1993. Raikes bears by Applause. 13in (33cm) tall;
(Left) Allison. White acrylic fur; carved wooden face and foot pads; inset plastic eyes; jointed arms and legs; swivel head. Dressed in blue and mauve dress with matching bow at ear and white pantaloons trimmed with lace. Style number 54382. Limited edition of 7500.
(Right) Alec. Brown acrylic fur; carved wooden face and foot pads; inset plastic eyes; jointed arms and legs; swivel head. Dressed in brown pants with brown suspenders, long sleeve white shirt with floral bow tie. Style number 54382. Limited edition of 7500. A wicker picnic basket accompanies bears. Sold as a set.
Courtesy Applause.

Jasper and Jessica. First Edition Puppies. 1992. Raikes puppies by Applause. 12in (31cm) tall;
(Left) Jasper. Light brown acrylic fur; carved wooden face and foot pads; inset plastic eyes; jointed arms and legs; swivel head. Dressed in blue sailor suit trimmed in red with red and white striped undershirt. Signed and numbered. Style number 52496. Limited edition of 5000.
(Right) Jessica. Light brown acrylic fur; carved wooden face and foot pads; inset plastic eyes; jointed arms and legs; swivel head. Dressed in red dress with white collar and red bow on her head. Signed and numbered. Style number 52505. Limited edition of 7500.
Courtesy Applause.

Tom Sawyer and Becky Thatcher. 1993. Raikes bears by Applause. 19in (48cm) tall;
(Left) Becky Thatcher. Medium brown acrylic fur; carved wooden face and foot pads; inset plastic eyes; jointed arms and legs; swivel head. Dressed in blue and white plaid dress with a matching bow on her head; ecru eyelet petticoat trimmed with blue ribbon with matching pantaloons. Signed and numbered. Style number 38584. Limited edition of 5000.
(Right) Tom Sawyer. Medium brown acrylic fur; carved wooden face and foot pads; inset plastic eyes; jointed arms and legs; swivel head. Dressed in blue and white striped pants; blue shirt; blue and white plaid handkerchief around neck and straw hat. Carries a fishing pole with wooden fish dangling from line. Signed and numbered. Style number 38585. Limited edition of 5000.
Courtesy Ed and Liz Oerding.

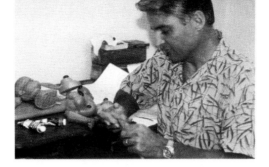

Bob, working on a prototype for Applause in his studio.

Chapter Six

The Creation of a Robert Raikes Teddy Bear

Robert Raikes has been called the "modern day Gepetto," after the famed creator of Pinocchio. He loves to carve and approaches each piece of wood as if it were a new adventure. His imagination, hard work and attention to detail have earned him the reputation of being one of America's most successful and admired teddy bear artists today.

Being involved in the world of teddy bears for so many years myself, I appreciate how collectors thirst for information about their hobby. I have found the more learned about the area in which one collects, the more interesting the hobby becomes.

So I asked Bob to share with us how he creates his famous Raikes teddy bears.

"When I first get an inspiration for a new design, I go to my drawing board and quickly make a rough sketch. By working fast,I let my feelings really flow onto the paper. There is no need for fine detail at this point, as I feel it slows down your creativity. I make progressive drawings. For example, on one page I will sketch the first design of a bear, then I'll draw the same sketch, only this time maybe give the bear a tongue, then onto the next sketch changing the dimensions somewhat.

"After I feel satisfied with the final sketch, I draw half of the profile of my final design onto a piece of tracing paper. To be sure the face is symmetrical, I fold the paper in half, so now when I begin working with the clay, my background is perfectly matched. Placing a ball of clay onto my drawing, I draw a line down the center of the clay for a guide. Not paying much attention to the drawing at this point, I begin the creative process of working on the face. Once I get the basic look and proportions, I compare the picture with the clay and decide which I like better.

"Once the main design is completed, I make my hard copy in wood. After finely sanding, any necessary corrections are made. Then, I recarve some parts and do the final detail work. The eyes are glued in place, and the features are then carefully painted. Finally, I apply a clear protective coat.

"For each carved wooden prototype I make for Applause, I also make a resin copy from the original clay sculpture. In some cases it may be necessary to grind or add resin to the copy until I am completely satisfied with the design. The resin copy gives the exact proportions and allows Applause to put the hard copy on their machine. The wooden prototype gives the coloration. I complete and dress the body so Applause can see exactly how the finished product should look.

"Sometimes, the Applause prototype goes back and forth between me and Applause before I give my final approval. I must be satisfied with the Applause version of my work and that it represents my original.

"This procedure can take up to six months before the piece is finally ready for production. Applause normally likes to have my designs at least one year in advance. However, I am now working several years ahead with my designs. Mentally, I'm five years ahead."

Bob concluded our interview by saying laughingly, "I only hope my work continues to sell as well as it is now so I may use all these ideas I have."

When Robert Raikes first gets an inspiration for a new design, he goes to his drawing board and quickly makes a rough sketch. Here he is seen making these first progressive drawings.

Chapter Seven

Young Kerianne Mills (age five) was overjoyed to have Robert Raikes personally sign her Sherwood *at my San Diego Teddy Bear, Doll and Antique Toy Festival in 1988. Robert Raikes autographed over 1600 of his bears that day.* Courtesy of Georgann Mills.

Robert Raikes' Philosophy of Life

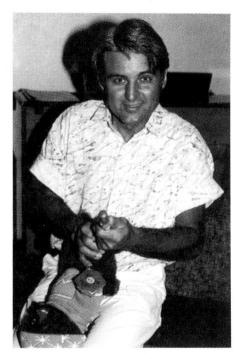

When I first invited Robert Raikes to autograph his creations at my San Diego Teddy Bear, Doll and Antique Toy Festival in 1986, the talented artist "hand-carved" his signature on the foot of hundreds of his bears manufactured by Applause.

From the very first time I met Robert Raikes at a doll show at the Anaheim Convention Center in California in 1982, he gave me the feeling of a person who not only cared about his work, but sincerely cared about people.

Busy as he was the day of the show, surrounded by collectors wanting to buy his wonderful creations, he would take time to talk to each individual, letting them know that everyone of them was very special to him, and he was sincerely interested in their questions and remarks.

Basically, Robert Raikes is a very shy, soft-spoken person. His father recalls how nervous his son was when talking to people about his work. "I really had to persuade Bob to do shows, as he was really shy," explained Mr. Raikes Sr. "He would always stand in the background and watch. When collectors would ask who the artist was, I would point to my son and say, 'there he is,' and young Bob would immediately take off."

I appreciated Bob's talent as a sculptor from the time I saw his work. Bob and Carol exhibited their own work when I produced my first Teddy Bear and Antique Toy Festival in San Diego, California, in 1983. I feel very proud to have had them as a part of this very special event in my life.

After Bob and Carol entered into the contract with the gift company of Applause, I witnessed incredible reactions to the Raikes bears. I had the idea to invite the popular artist and his wife, Carol, to be guests at my 1986 San Diego Teddy Bear and Antique Toy Festival. I proposed he would autograph his bears by Applause and demonstrate his carving talents. As this would be Bob's first signing at a show, it took quite a lot of persuasion on my part before the shy artist consented. I anticipated a good response at the show from Bob and Carol's appearance, but my estimation was far below the crowds of collectors that stood in line for hours with their arms full of bears.

One lady appeared with a baby buggy overflowing with Raikes bears. Many collectors' cars were jammed full of bears to be signed. One of the most amazing things to me about those early signings was that Bob actually hand-carved his name on the foot of each bear. Bob carved his name on over 1500 bears that day. He signed from 10 a.m. to 4 p.m. with no break, even for lunch. I asked him, "How can you even hold a carving tool for that long?" He smiled saying, "I can carve my name almost as fast as I can write with a pen."

I have been very fortunate to have Bob appear at my San Diego festivals for four years to date. With each signing, hundreds more men, women and children of all ages appear at the show, unable to resist the appeal of the Raikes bears. They are now avid collectors. However, it is not just the bears that have won the hearts of collectors, but the artist himself. His warm, caring attitude has brought him almost as much fame as his bears. Bob lets people know they are important to him and they return this feeling. I have watched Bob at shows patiently listening to collectors endless questions, stories and looking at numerous pictures of their Raikes bear collections.

When I began research for this book, Bob and his wife, Carol, kindly invited my husband and me to spend a weekend with them at their house in Mount Shasta, California. This enabled me to not only photograph Bob's original work, but to interview the couple in the relaxed atmosphere of their home.

It was a beautiful, crystal clear fall day when we arrived. The smell of the giant California pine trees was so refreshing, I could easily see why Bob would get his inspirations by living in this tranquil, natural mountain setting. The weekend I spent at the Raikes' home was not only lots of fun, but a very memorable and inspiring experience.

We got up early in the morning, as we planned to photograph Bob's original work in the pristine, verdant setting of Mount Shasta. I gazed out of the window just in time to see Bob taking off for his early morning bike ride. This daily event in Bob's life is not

One of Bob's favorite pastimes is his early morning bike ride. This daily event in his life is not only one of his favorites, but he says it clears his mind and gives him time to prepare for his full day ahead in his studio.

only one of his favorites, but he said it clears his mind and gives him time to prepare for his full day ahead in his studio.

We all had so much fun that day photographing the bears. With the enthusiasm and the excitement of young children, we all romped through the woods, finding the ideal spot to photograph Bob's wonderful bears and animals. We even risked our lives climbing the huge mountain rocks and jumping over the fast flowing rivers to get that ideal picture. That evening, tired but happy and pleased with the achievements of the day, we sat in the cozy den of Bob and Carol's home. I was not only warmed by the huge, crackling fire, but the warmth shared by the Raikes family. Their own daughters, Jenny (ten) and Emily (eight), were extremely interested in my authoring a book about their father's work and their family.

Bob expressed the importance of letting his children feel their involvement. "When we were making the dolls and bears, before they went anywhere, they had to be inspected by the children." Bob admits Jenny and Emily were their strongest critics. "They thought that all the dolls and bears were theirs. I think they must believe they live in Santa's house. The dolls and bears are an integral part of our lives. Our children are always around our work and for them it's normal to have bears and dolls all over our dining room and kitchen tables."

It is an everyday sight to see the children sitting watching television with the bears and dolls all around them. A precious sight the evening we were there was that of young Emily, curled up into the arms of Bob's huge 5ft (152cm) original bear. "Ever since she was a little girl, this has been one of her favorite places to sit at night," Bob said.

Bob's concern for the plight of people less fortunate than himself leads him to Mexicali, Mexico, each year. With friends and family, they volunteer their time and talents to help bring a better life to the residents of Mexicali. Bob is pictured here with some of the children that live in Mexicali. Courtesy Robert and Carol Raikes.

Jenny was delighted when her father created a set of bears named after his children. Here Jenny happily shows off the finished products of Jenny *(left) and* Jason *(right). Courtesy of Robert and Carol Raikes.*

I found Carol to be everything everyone told me about her—sweet, reserved, soft-spoken and a devoted wife and mother. She was reluctant to discuss her invaluable contribution to Bob's career. She never mentioned how hard she worked and the loyal support she had given her husband during those long hard years, but instead, focused on the good times and their plans for the future. Since signing the contract with Applause, Carol no longer has to help Bob with his work. Therefore, she devotes all her time to her family.

Bob and Carol shared so much of their life with me that weekend. It was Bob's philosophy of life that impressed me the most. He told of the hard times and how much he and Carol had sacrificed to reach the point where they were today. He said it was a growing period for them and they were both stronger and learned so much from those experiences. "When I was young," Bob recalls, "like most young men my age, I wanted to change the world. Actually, I'm still trying to do it. I know I can't change it, but I do plan to make a lot of people happy. I think the whole reason I got into art in the first place was not only to do creative work and do something special with my life, but I wanted to show people I cared about them. We live in a society that is much too fast. There is very little caring out there. My first and most important goal with my work is to try and bring a little joy into the world. I have a basic Christian philosophy of caring for others, and I sincerely try to put that feeling in my work. People really do come first with me. Carol and I have had to go without a lot for over a decade. If I had wanted to cut corners and not show I cared through my work, I could have made it in different ways with my artwork. But, I wasn't willing to do that."

Bob's voice was firm but very sincere as he told me this. "It's only amusing in retrospect, but we have lost many a night's sleep when we were making our dolls and bears. We'd driven long distances in one day to do a show, getting up at three o'clock in the morning and not getting back until eleven o'clock at night. We did this to avoid paying for a motel which, fortunately, we do not have to worry about as much anymore."

I asked Bob what advice he could give to the artists just beginning. "Just put all your heart and energy into your work." He went on to say how he feels he wasted a lot of years

A precious sight the evening I visited the Raikes home was that of Bob's young daughter, Emily, curled up into the arms of Bob's huge 5ft (152cm) original bear.

Robert Raikes Sr and his wife, Cathy, opened up their home and their hearts to me during my 1988 visit. They allowed me to photograph their whole collection and answered endless questions regarding their son's work.

going in different directions. "Try to be systematic and professional. I wish I had learned more about the business world in the beginning. You need to have people around you that are both encouraging and critical and help you with your work. If you believe in yourself and know where you're going, you can make it. It is so rewarding for me to know there are approximately 80,000 of my products out there, sitting on shelves throughout the world making people smile on a daily basis. It's so easy to make people happy," said Bob smiling. "If I can make people happy with just a teddy bear, think what people can do with a lot more talent and insight than me. I had no formal art training. My success comes from a God-given gift, an inner peace and an insight that I feel helps me put joy in my work."

On the return journey home from my memorable weekend in Mount Shasta with Bob Raikes and his family, I had the pleasure of visiting the home of Bob's parents, Robert Raikes Sr. and his wife, Cathy. They lived in the beautiful coastal town of Los Osos, California. I was overwhelmed when I walked into their home with their collection of Bob's original work. It was virtually a Robert Raikes museum.

Cathy smiled and explained how several of the pieces in their collection were discarded prototypes that did not satisfy their son. She went on to tell me how she had managed to rescue them before the salvage truck came and these rare pieces of her son's work would have been gone forever.

It was soon apparent the sculptor's warm and sensitive personality was part of his heritage. Mr. Raikes Sr. and his wife were truly two of the most genuine, wonderful people I have ever met.

Their faces beamed with pride as they related events in their son's successful career.

I was delighted to find they had saved several of the very first dolls and teddy bears Bob created, and many additional examples of his early carvings. What originally was only to be an afternoon at Bob's parents house turned into two full days.

Robert Raikes Sr. and Cathy opened up their home and their hearts to me, allowing me to photograph their whole collection and answering my endless questions regarding their son's work.

Cathy and Robert Raikes Sr.

Chapter Eight

Care and Repair of Raikes Bears

A subject that is of great interest to Raikes collectors is how to care for and restore these treasured and valuable possessions. Dan and Jan Mitzel have been avid Raikes collectors for many years and became interested in restoring Raikes bears and animals several years ago. I asked them to share with us some of these valuable tips.

"We all love our bears, rabbits, raccoons, and the rest of our menagerie. But sometimes no matter how precious THEY are or how careful YOU are, accidents will happen. Perhaps an admirer was holding one and let him slip or worse yet, an overly jealous pet decided to take his revenge! It has happened to the best of us (our family included!). That particular bear has become too much a part of the family to just let go of and too expensive to replace! It's at this point when you begin to get creative. Did you know that a warm damp sponge held on that little dent where your precious one hit the fireplace mantle may actually cause the wood to swell up and make the injury hardly noticeable? We have discovered this and several other little tricks over the years.

"Minor scratches can be repaired quite easily. Raikes animals have been made with many different types of woods and stains. Some have been made without any stain at all. In this case, you may be able to lightly buff the scratched area with a very fine steel wool and apply a thin coat of varnish to obtain the desired effect.

"If the scratch is on a painted surface such as the nose or eyebrows but has not damaged the wood, lightly sand the area then use a matching color of artist oils to blend the surface. You may have to mix your own color to match.

"Each animal has a slightly different color, this is part of what makes it unique. If a scratch occurs on the lighter surfaces of the animal such as the face or foot, use linseed oil to thin the paint after you have mixed the color. Thinning the paint will make it act like a stain and allow the wood grain to show through. Trying to mix stains together to achieve a desired color is next to impossible since they were not designed for this purpose.

"If the scratch is quite deep, you may need to use a neutral colored wood putty to fill the scratch before you paint. By doing this, you will most likely lose some of the wood grain. When this happens, you can create the look of wood grain by using a thin brush and darker color to paint in the appearance of wood grain lines to insure a perfect match on the lighter surfaces.

"After the paint has had a minimum of three days to dry, apply one coat of varnish. When purchasing the varnish, make sure you get the SATIN finish. Allow the varnish to dry overnight. Lightly buff the varnish with very fine steel wool. Remove all dust particles and then apply a second coat of varnish.

"Don't try to use furniture polishes which contain stains. They will only highlight the problem area because these products are generally made for dark colors and most of the Raikes animals have light colored wood.

"When you are working with the damaged animal, be sure to protect the fur and clothing. Most of the clothing is easily removed. To protect the fur, place the entire animal in a plastic bag and use elastic bands to secure the plastic around the area to be worked on.

These techniques can be used for most minor repairs. You may need the help of a skilled craftsman if the animal is severely damaged. Don't try to use wood putty to cover large areas. Be patient and don't give up! Good luck!"

A Chronology of Robert Raikes

1947 — Born October 13, in Van Nuys, California. Son of Robert and Cathy Raikes.

1968 to 1970 — Served in the United States Navy.

1970 — August 15, married Carol Morris.

1970 — Began wood sculpting after being inspired by Gilbert Valencia, chief carver for the Weatherby Rifle Company.

1973 to 1976 — Attended California Polytechnical College.

1973 to 1978 — Lived in Morro Bay.

1974 — Joined the National Carvers' Association.

1974 — May 23, first child, Jason, was born.

1974 to 1976 — Taught carving at Adult Education classes and at several high schools.

1974 to 1976 — Continued wood carving as a full-time profession, sculpting from mantels and headboards to figures and animals.

1975 — Created the first dolls, under the name of "Little Wooden Children."

1978 — Moved to Grass Valley, California.

1978 — October 9, second child, Jenny, was born.

1980 — Moved to Mt. Shasta, California.

1980 — April 19, Emily was born.

1981 — Won award in the "Fly Away" contest for best novice carver.

1981 — Commissioned to carve two life-size carousel horses by Holiday Inn in Santa Margarita, California.

1981 — Exhibited at first doll show in Santa Rosa, California.

1981 to 1983 — Concentrated on making dolls.

1982 — Began creating teddy bears under the name of *Woody Bear*.

1982 — Doll becomes more sophisticated. With the introduction of the dolls with all hand-carved wooden bodies, Bob changed the name of his creations to "Raikes Originals."

1984 — October, unable to meet the increasing demand for his products, Bob signed a contract with the well-known gift company Applause to produce his creations. In the agreement, Bob was still able to produce special order bears under the name *Woody Bear*.

1987 — October 13, Bob's 40th birthday, the artist made the decision that a good portion of his original work will be produced especially for special events, competitions, various charities and the Robert Raikes Collector's Club.

1988 — May, The Good Company becomes a division of Applause, Inc.

1988 — June, the Robert Raikes Collector's Club is formed.

1988 — December 6-11, appeared as a celebrity guest at the First Annual Walt Disney World Teddy Bear Convention in Florida.

1989 — October 13-15, the First National Convention of the Robert Raikes Collector's Club held in Woodland Hills, California.

1989 — November 28-December 6, appeared as a celebrity guest at the Walt Disney World's Showcase of Dolls and Second Annual Teddy Bear Convention in Florida.

1989 — December 7, Applause and The Good Company consolidate, creating one full-line gift company-Applause, Inc.

1990 — September 14-16, RRCC 2nd Annual Convention, Nashville, Tennessee, "Calico Pete At The Grand Ole Opry."

— November 29-December 2, appeared as a celebrity guest at the 3rd Annual Walt Disney World® Teddy Bear Convention in Florida.

1991 — May 18-25, RRCC 3rd Annual Convention, Tropical Fantasy, a Caribbean Cruise.

— October 13, Bob is guest artist for Merbears By the Sea Convention, in Lincoln City, Oregon.

— December 4th, RRCC mini-convention in Florida, at the Stouffer Orlando Resort.

— December 5-8, appeared as a special guest at the Walt Disney World® Teddy Bear Convention in Orlando, Florida.

1992 — 1992 marks the first year that Bob did not do a signing tour, and it was also the beginning of the annual memberships for the RRCC.

— January 1st, RRCC annual memberships begin.

— June 18-21, appeared as a celebrity guest at the 1st Annual Disneyland Teddy Bear Classic Convention in Anaheim, California. Bob's 25 pieces were sold in seconds.

— July 31-August 2, RRCC 4th Annual Convention in Seattle, Washington.

— December 3-6, appeared as a celebrity guest at the Walt Disney World® Teddy Bear Convention in Florida.

1993 — Bob resumes a busy signing schedule and also makes plans to start his own company.

— April 29-May 2, appeared as a celebrity guest at the 2nd Annual Disneyland Teddy Bear & Doll Classic Convention in Anaheim, California. Some people waited approximately 48 hours to purchase the eight Raikes originals.

— The RRCC passes its five year anniversary with over 6,000 club members on its roster.

— June 1st, RRCC lifetime memberships are no longer accepted.

— October 22-24, RRCC 5th Annual Convention in Lancaster, Pennsylvania.

Robert Raikes Bear & Doll Price Guide

by
Linda Mullins

Copyright 1993 Linda Mullins

Introduction

Collecting Robert Raikes creations is increasing in popularity every year. The large number of collectors entering this field inspired me to write the price guide.

Robert Raikes has been creating his original dolls since 1975 and his bears since 1982, and these pieces have appreciated considerably.

But in 1984, when Robert Raikes was unable to meet the increasing demand for his products, he signed a contract with the major gift and licensing company, Applause, Inc., to produce his creations. By Applause, Inc. producing limited editions, this still kept Raikes' work highly select, but enabled many more collectors the opportunity to purchase his work. Applause does not solely produce limited editions, but does control the flow of Raikes' products, keeping them relatively valuable.

The Applause bears designed by Robert Raikes were an instant success. The impact they made on the collector's market was unbelievable. They appreciated in price at an outstanding rate.

The prices in this guide have been determined by studying shows, auctions, printed advertising, prices in newspapers and magazines. By examining the current market as well as price trends over the last year, I have done my very utmost to bring you the most up-to-date prices to the best of my ability.

Prices on Raikes "originals" are not included when not enough have been sold to establish a consistent price/value on the piece.

However, the current values in this booklet should only be used as a guide. The establishment of value must be yours in the end.

Prices may vary due to dealer philosophy and even the fancy of a collector. For instance, an informed and well-invested collector may choose to pay much more than book value for a piece because it completes a set. Or it may be that a collector attends an auction and simply dearly covets a particular piece. So those and similar situations cannot be taken into account when regarding the average bear.

Similarly, this guide is not meant to set prices from one section of the country to another. For instance, California prices for Raikes' work appear to be the highest.

Since prices are greatly influenced by condition as well as demand, please note that prices given in this guide are for pieces in excellent condition or, in the case of Raikes creations produced by Applause or The Good Company, the price would include the original collector box and certificate.

In various instances, the animals and dolls in the illustrations referred to in the price guide will have been personally autographed by Robert Raikes. However, the prices given in the guide are for pieces not personally autographed by Robert Raikes.

Neither the author nor the publisher assumes responsibility for any losses which may occur as a result of issuing this guide.

Whether you are an experienced or novice collector of Robert Raikes' work, I hope this price guide will aid you when considering purchasing or selling his bears and/or dolls.

Collecting Robert Raikes creations is a fun and exciting hobby, but if you wish to become more knowledgeable and deepen your understanding of his remarkable work, it requires a lot of study and self-education.

With this price guide (coupled with my book *The Raikes Bear & Doll Story*), your hobby will hopefully become ultimately more satisfying and rewarding.

Robert Raikes Creations By Applause Price Guide

Page Number	Original Retail Price	1993 Price Guide	Name	Style Number	Size
			First Edition: Autumn 1985 7500 Pieces Each		
78	$100	$ 725-up	Rebecca	#5447	22in (56cm)
78	$100	$ 300-up	Sebastian	#5445	22in (56cm)
78	$ 65	$ 300-up	Bently	#5448	14in (36cm)
78	$ 65	$1000-up	Chelsea	#5451	14in (36cm)
78	$ 65	$ 600-up	Eric	#5449	14in (36cm)
79	$100	$ 300-up	Huckle Bear	#5446	22in (56cm)
			Autumn 1985 Unnumbered Pieces		
79	$ 20	$ 95-up	Jamie (Brown and Gray)	#5453	10in (25cm)
79	$ 35	$ 150-up	Sherwood (Light Brown and Dark Brown)	#5452	13in (33cm)
			Second Edition: Spring 1986 15,000 Pieces Each		
81	$100	$ 225-up	Kitty	#5458	24in (61cm)
81	$100	$ 250-up	Max	#5460	24in (61cm)
81	$ 65	$ 375-up	Christopher	#5455	16in (41cm)
81	$ 65	$ 575-up	Penelope	#5457	16in (41cm)
81	$100	$ 250-up	Arnold	#5459	24in (61cm)
82	$ 65	$ 375-up	Benjamin	#5456	16in (41cm)
82	$300	$ 725-up	Tyrone*	#5461	36in (91cm)

* Only 5000 pieces

Page Number	Original Retail Price	1993 Price Guide	Name	Style Number	Size
			Wedding Couple Summer 1986 10,000 Pairs		
82	$150/pair	$ 600/pair	Gregory**	#5462	16in (41cm)
82			Allison**	#5462	16in (41cm)

**Numbered to 15,000 pairs
   Only 10,000 pairs made

Page Number	Original Retail Price	1993 Price Guide	Name	Style Number	Size
			Third Edition: Glamour Bears of the 1920s Autumn 1986 15,000 Pieces Each		
83	$100	$ 725-up	Lindy	#5463	24in (61cm)
83	$ 65	$ 200-up	Reginald	#5467	16in (41cm)
83	$ 65	$ 225-up	Daisy	#5468	16in (41cm)
84	$100	$ 250-up	Maude	#5464	24in (61cm)
84	$ 65	$ 495-up	Zelda	#5465	16in (41cm)
84	$ 65	$ 175-up	Cecil	#5466	16in (41cm)
			First Edition: Rabbits Spring 1987 Unnumbered Pieces		
84	$ 75	$ 450-up	Rebecca*	#20136	18in (46cm)
84	$ 75	$ 450-up	Calvin**	#20137	18in (46cm)

*Rebecca: Total of 5000 pieces produced to date
**Calvin: Total of 5000 pieces produced to date

Page Number	Original Retail Price	1993 Price Guide	Name	Style Number	Size
			Fourth Edition: Americana Collection Spring 1987 7500 Pieces Each		
85	$100	$ 175-up	Miss Melony	#17005	24in (61cm)
85	$ 65	$ 175-up	Sara Anne	#17002	16in (41cm)
85	$ 65	$ 250-up	Margaret	#17004	16in (41cm)
85	$ 65	$ 250-up	Casey	#17003	16in (41cm)
			Second Edition: Rabbits Spring 1988 5000 Pieces Each		
86	$ 75	$ 225-up	Jill	#20266	23in (58cm)
86	$ 75	$ 225-up	Andrew	#20267	23in (58cm)
			Timber Creek Collection (Beavers) Spring 1988 5000 Each		
87	$ 75	$ 100-up	Sam	#17012	14in (36cm)
87	$ 75	$ 100-up	Lucy	#17011	14in (36cm)
			Fifth Edition: Sweet Sunday Collection Spring 1988 7500 Pieces Each		
88	$ 75	$ 200-up	Sally	#17007	16in (41cm)
88	$ 75	$ 200-up	Susie	#17008	16in (41cm)
88	$ 75	$ 150-up	Timmy	#17009	16in (41cm)
			Summer 1988 Unnumbered Pieces		
89	$ 28	$ 45-up	Terry (White and Brown)	#17010	12in (31cm)

Total of 15,000 pieces produced to date

Page Number	Original Retail Price	1993 Price Guide	Name	Style Number	Size
		Sixth Edition: Home Sweet Home Collection Summer 1988 10,000 Pieces Each			
90	$125	$ 150-up	Emily	#17013	26in (66cm)
90	$ 80	$ 125-up	Jason	#17015	18in (46cm)
90	$ 80	$ 175-up	Jenny	#17014	18in (46cm)
		Autumn 1988 10,000 Pieces			
91	$ 75	$ 90-up	Kevi (Comes with Kevin Roth Tape)	#17019	12in (31cm)
		Christmas 1988 7500 Pieces Each			
91	$100	$ 225-up	Santa	#21390	17in (43cm)
91	$100	$225-up	Mrs. Clause	#21391	17in (43cm)
		Third Edition: Rabbits Easter 1989 7500 Pieces Each			
92	$ 85	$ 125-up	Mr. Nickleby	#20399	16in (41cm)
92	$ 85	$ 125-up	Mrs. Nickleby	#20398	16in (41cm)
		Rabbits Easter 1989 Unnumbered Pieces			
92	$ 30	$ 60-up	Ashley	#20400	11in (28cm)
92	$ 30	$ 60-up	Brett	#20401	11in (28cm)
Total of 15,000 produced to date					
		Seventh Edition: Saturday Matinee Collection Spring 1989 10,000 Pieces Each			
93	$ 75	$ 175-up	Lionel	#17023	18in (46cm)
93	$ 75	$ 125-up	Bonnie	#17022	18in (46cm)
93	$ 75	$ 125-up	Jesse	#17021	18in (46cm)
		First Edition: Mother's Day 1989 7500 Pieces			
94	$ 80	$ 250-up	Annie	#660283	16in (41cm)
		Spring 1989 Unnumbered Pieces			
96	$ 28	$ 35-up	Cookie Bear (Gray and Brown)	#660330	12in (31cm)
Total of 30,000 pieces produced to date					
		First Edition Dolls: Spring 1989 7500 Pieces Each			
96	$125	$ 125-up	Molly	#660284	16in (41cm)
96	$150	$ 150-up	Juliet	#660285	14in (36cm)
		Sherwood Forest Collection: Spring 1989 7500 Pieces Each			
97	$ 95	$ 110-up	Robin Raccoon	#660331	16in (41cm)
97	$ 95	$ 110-up	Marion Hedgehog	#660332	20in (51cm)
		Summer 1989 10,000 Pieces			
97	$ 90	$ 110	Liza	#660376	13in (33cm)
		Christmas 1989 7500 Pieces			
97	$100	$ 225-up	Santa	#660334	14in (36cm)
		Christmas 1989 Unnumbered Series			
97	$ 40	$ 70-up	Elves (Green, Red)	#660335	12in (31cm)
		Three Bears on Wooden Base Autumn 1989 7500 Sets			
98	$220	$ 240-up/set	Three Bears	#661434	12in (31cm)
		Fourth Edition: Rabbits Spring 1990 7500 Pieces Each			
	$ 85		Aunt Mary Lou	#661416	12in (31cm)
	$ 85		Uncle Vincent	#661427	12in (31cm)
	$ 40		Betsy Ann	#661428	8in (20cm)
	$ 40		Vincent, Jr.	#661429	8in (20cm)
		Eighth Edition: Camp Grizzly Collection Spring 1990 7500 Pieces Each			
99	$ 90		Hillary	#661431	16in (41cm)
99	$130		Wendall	#661430	24in (61cm)
99	$ 90		Jeremy	#661432	16in (41cm)
		First Edition: Valentine's Day Spring 1990 Unnumbered Pieces			
100	$ 40		Sophie	#661380	12in (31cm)
		Second Edition: Mother's Day 1990 7500 Pieces Each			
	$135/set		Charlotte	#661433	11in (28cm)
			Toby	#661433	6in (15cm)

Page Number	Original Retail Price	1993 Price Guide	Name	Style Number	Size
			Spring 1990 10,000 Pieces		
	$ 85		Courtney	#662027	12in (31cm)
			Nursery Miniatures Spring 1990 10,000+ Pieces Each		
	$ 36		Lisa Marie	#38518	7in (18cm)
	$ 36		Nathan	#38519	7in (18cm)
	$ 36		Ben	#38520	7in (18cm)
	$ 36		Allison	#38521	7in (18cm)
	$ 36		Robbie	#38522	7in (18cm)
	$ 36		Mitzi	#38523	7in (18cm)
			Ninth Edition: The Royal Court Autumn 1990 10,000 Pieces Each		
100	$180		King William	#662347	22in (56cm)
	$180		Queen Mary	#662348	22in (56cm)
	$110		Court Jester	#662349	14in (36cm)
			Christmas 1990 10,000 Pieces		
	$110		Classic Santa	#662031	12in (31cm)
			Snowdomes Christmas 1990 10,000 Pieces Each		
	$ 45		Tyrone & Kitty	#38510	5½in (14cm)
	$ 45		Sally, Susie & Timmy	#38512	5½in (14cm)
	$ 45		Eric	#38513	5½in (14cm)
	$ 45		Penelope	#38514	5½in (14cm)
			Fifth Edition: Rabbits Spring 1991		
	$180/pair		Mrs. Hopkins*	#53048	10in (25cm)
			Mr. Hopkins*	#53048	10in (25cm)
	$ 36		Cambria**	#53049	8½in (21cm)
	$ 36		Daniel**	#53050	8½in (21cm)

*The Hopkins: Limited Edition 10,000 pieces each
**Cabria and Daniel: Unnumbered pieces

Page Number	Original Retail Price	1993 Price Guide	Name	Style Number	Size
			Second Edition: Valentine's Day July 1991 1800 Pieces		
	$ 50		Cupid Bear	#662265	11in (28cm)
			Tenth Edition: Best Friends Collection Spring 1991 10,000 Pieces		
101	$120		Brian	#38516	16in (41cm)
			Sport	#38516	4½in (5cm)
101	$120		Stacie	#38517	16in (41cm)
			Fifi	#38517	4½in (5cm)
			First Father's Day Edition: Spring 1991 Unnumbered Pieces		
	$50		Papa Bear	#54191	12in (31cm)
			Third Edition: Mother's Day 1991 10,000 Pieces Each		
	$140		Lucille & Daphne (sold as set)	#54122	12in (31cm)
					7in (18cm)
			Summer 1991 Unnumbered Pieces		
	$38		Playtime Cookie	#38568	12in (31cm)
			Second Edition Dolls: 1991 7500 Pieces each		
	$150		Claire	#38546	12in (31cm)
	$150		Abigail	#38547	12in (31cm)
			Summer 1991 Unnumbered Pieces		
	$45		Woody Bear	#38509	12in (31cm)
			Fourth Edition: Christmas 1991 10,000 Pieces Each		
13	$100		Nicolette	#51243	16in (41cm)
			Eleventh Edition: Flying High Winter 1991 10,000 Pieces Each		
101	$75		Lindy, Jr.	#38556	12in (31cm)
	$75		Amelia	#38557	12in (31cm)
			Valentine Edition: Summer 1992 Unnumbered Pieces		
	$70		George and Gracie (sold as set) (Comes with loveseat)	#52257	7in (18cm)

Page Number	Original Retail Price	1993 Price Guide	Name	Style Number	Size
			Sixth Edition: Rabbits Spring 1992 7500 Pieces Each		
	$90		Paulette	#53249	15½in (39cm)
			Mother's Day Autumn 1992 7500 Pieces Each		
102	$70		Sidney (cat)	#38558	12in (31cm)
	$70		Charmaine (cat)	#38559	12in (31cm)
			Wedding Set (Second Edition) Spring 1992 7500 Pieces Each		
103	$70		Bob and Carol (sold as set)	#38577	7in (18cm)
			Christmas 1992 7500 Pieces Each		
102	$125		Santa Bear	#51488	19in (48cm)
	$100		Kathie Bear	#51489	16in (41cm)
			Spring 1992 1500 Pieces Each		
102	$180		Diamond Jim Brady	#38586	21in (53cm)
	$180		Ruby the Dance Hall Girl	#38587	21in (53cm)
			Rabbits Easter 1993 7500 Pieces Each		
	$70		Dottie	#53416	12in (31cm)
	$70		Dylan	#53417	12in (31cm)
			Autumn 1992 7500 Pieces Each		
104	$70		Jasper (puppy)	#52496	12in (31cm)
	$70		Jessica (puppy)	#52505	12in (31cm)
			"The Picnic Pair" 1993 7500 Pieces Each		
104	$175		Allison and Alec (sold as set)	#54382	13in (33cm)
			Spring 1993 5000 Pieces Each		
104	$125		Tom Sawyer	#38585	19in (48cm)
	$125		Becky Thatcher	#38584	19in (48cm)

Robert Raikes Collector Club Bears

Page Number	Original Retail Price	1993 Price Guide	Name	Style Number	Size
			First Edition: Summer 1988 Unnumbered Pieces		
11	$65		Terry (black) (included RRCC membership)	#17010	12in (31cm)
			Second Edition: Spring 1990 Unnumbered Pieces		
11	$70		Panda Bear	#30303	11in (28cm)
			Third Edition: Spring 1992 Unnumbered Pieces		
11	$50		Tammy	#30378	7in (18cm)

Robert Raikes Collector's Club Convention Bears

Page Number	Original Retail Price	1993 Price Guide	Name	Style Number	Size
			First Edition: Winter 1989 2500 Pieces Each		
12	$200	$450	Pirates of the Pacific (Bill Buccaneer and M'Lady Honeypot) (sold as set)	#30178	12in (31cm)
			Second Edition: Autumn 1990 - 1500 Pieces Each		
12	$185	$250	Calico Pete	#30304	17in (43cm)
			Third Edition: Spring 1991 10,000 Pieces Each		
12	$160	$160	Savannah	#30324	10in (25cm)
			Fourth Edition: Summer 1992 250 Pieces Each		
13	$160	$450	Petunia	#30643	18in (46cm)
			Fifth Edition: Fall 1993 500 Pieces Each		
13	$375		Jacob and Katie (sold as a set)		18in (46cm)

Page Number	Original Retail Price	1993 Price Guide	Name	Style Number	Size

Robert Raikes Walt Disney World® Convention Bears

Page Number	Original Retail Price	1993 Price Guide	Name	Style Number	Size
14	$125	$350	First Edition: Winter 1989 100 Pieces Each Terry (black acrylic fur) Dressed in T-shirt (included RRCC membership)	#170101	12in (31cm)
15	$195	$400	Second Edition: Winter 1990 500 Pieces Each Dolly and Her Rocking Horse (sold as set)	#40259	9in (23cm)
15	$185	$275	Third Edition: Winter 1991 500 Pieces Each Kris Kringle	#40304	12in (31cm)
15	$225	$500	Fourth Edition: Winter 1992 250 Pieces Each Mary Had A Little Lamb	#60050	19in (48cm)

Robert Raikes Disneyland Convention Bears

Page Number	Original Retail Price	1993 Price Guide	Name	Style Number	Size
2	$125	$500	First Edition: Spring 1992 25 Pieces Each Woody Bear Clown	#38509	12in (31cm)

Robert Raikes Collector's Club Special Editions

Page Number	Original Retail Price	1993 Price Guide	Name	Style Number	Size
13	$115	$275	Christmas 1991 300 Pieces Each Nicolette (Artist Proof)	#51243	16in (41cm)
2	$125	$400	Spring 1992 Unnumbered (35 Pieces Produced to Date) Woody Bear Clown #2	#38509	12in (31cm)
13	$125	$200	Summer 1992 1000 Pieces Each Francie	#30271	14in (36cm)

For Further Information...

Raikes Review, The Newsletter for Raikes Collectors

In 1989, a Raikes collector at a teddy bear show made the comment, "What we really need is a publication that is just about Raikes creations and targeted toward the serious collector." From that seed, the *Bearrister Bugle*, the newsletter for Raikes collectors, was born. Today, with the consent of artist Robert Raikes himself, *Bearrister Bugle*, is known as *Raikes Review* and has fast become the primary source of information among Raikes collectors.

Raikes Review is a publication dedicated exclusively to Raikes collecting. *Raikes Review* covers all aspects of Raikes collecting from a collector's viewpoint. *Raikes Review* editor, Michael Swindler, has been an avid Raikes collector since the first edition of Raikes bears was released by Applause in 1985. This bimonthly newsletter offers insightful features of interest to Raikes collectors.

Each issue also includes a focused and informative market report which analyzes both the secondary market and explores new releases.

Also regularly appearing in *Raikes Review* are collector profiles, a collectors mart to buy, sell and trade Raikes collectibles, letters to the editor, insightful editorial commentaries, not to mention original artwork and photographs that bring the world of Raikes collecting alive and provide an interesting look behind the scenes and into the making of original Raikes creations.

Raikes Review is proof that the treasured work of Robert Raikes has not only provided collectors with much enjoyment but has also become a vehicle for investments for many.

To help in that process, *Raikes Review* publishes its extremely popular Raikesranks, an analysis of every manufactured Raikes item released to date. Raikesranks accompanies every other issue of *Raikes Review* and fills two pages with market values of Raikes collectibles, recently revising its format in order to base values on the condition of the items.

In addition to all of the above, the publisher of *Raikes Review* also produces an annual supplement entitled *The Guide to Raikes Collectibles*. A complimentary copy of the *Guide* supplement is provided each year to subscribers of *Raikes Review*. The *Guide* is a complete chronological listing of manufactured Raikes releases.

All of this and more can be enjoyed with your annual subscription to *Raikes Review*, the newsletter for Raikes collectors. Upon receipt of your subscription request, the latest issue of *Raikes Review* and your complimentary copy of the most recent *Guide to Raikes Collectibles* supplement will be sent to you. Your initial issue will be followed every other month by five additional editions of the latest in Raikes information. Enclose your check or money order for $18 ($24 outside of the United States and Canada) and mail with your name and address to *Raikes Review*, P.O. Box 172, Hanover, Pennsylvania 17331.

Robert Raikes Original Bears & Dolls
Price Guide

Page Number	Name	Year	Description	Size	1993 Price Guide
DOLLS					
29	Pouty-face Boy Doll	1975	cloth body, carved wooden hair	27in (69cm)	$3500-up
31	Girl Doll "big-eyed" series	1981	cloth body, synthetic hair,	25in (64cm)	$3000-up
32	Clown Doll	1982	cloth body	22in (56cm)	$3800-up
34	(Left) Boy Doll	198	cloth body, hand-carved hair	23in (58cm)	$3500-up
36	Jester Doll	1984	all hand-carved wood, articulated head and body, brown feathers for hair	18in (46cm)	$4000-up
37	Girl Doll	1984	all hand-carved wood, articulated head and body, synthetic hair	26in (66cm)	$4500-up
BEARS					
48	Woody Bear	1983	burned wood effect	18in (46cm)	$3000-up
				24in (61cm)	$3500-up
49	Sherwood. Woody Bear	1983		14in (36cm)	$1200-up
49	Jamie. Woody Bear	1984		9.5in (23cm)	$ 950-up
52	Woody Bear	1984		20in (51cm)	$3000-up
55	Masque Face Ballerina Woody Bear	1984		18in (46cm)	$3500-up
61	Panda. Woody Bear	1986		24in (61cm)	$4500-up
62	Baby Bear. Woody Bear	1986		16in (41cm)	$2000-up
62	(Left) Chelsea-face Woody Bear	1986		18in (46cm)	$2200-up
	(Middle Left) Pouty-face Ballerina Woody Bear	1985		18in (46cm)	$2200-up
	(Middle Right) Sailor. Woody Bear	1985		18in (46cm)	$2500-up
	(Right) Pouty-face Woody Bear	1986		18in (46cm)	$2500-up
63	(Left) Swiss Girl. Woody Bear	1986		23in (58cm)	$3000-up
	(Center) Ballerina Woody Bear	1987		23in (58cm)	$3000-up
	(Right) Country Girl. Woody Bear	1986		23.5in (60cm)	$3000-up
63	Tyrone. Woody Bear	1986	dressed as a Scotsman	38in (97cm)	$4500-up
65	(Left) Train Engineer Woody Bear	1987		22in (56cm)	$3000-up
	(Center) Country Boy. Woody Bear	1986		23in (58cm)	$3000-up
	(Right) Swiss Boy. Woody Bear	1986		23in (58cm)	$3000-up
66	Kevi. Woody Bear	1987		14in (36cm)	$2000-up
66	Joey. Woody Bear	1987		12in (31cm)	$1000-up
68	(Left) Emily. Woody Bear	1988		24in (61cm)	$3000-up
	(Center) Jason. Woody Bear	1988		18in (46cm)	$1700-up
	(Right) Jenny. Woody Bear	1988		18in (46cm)	$1800-up
MISCELLANEOUS					
71	Rabbit (prototype)	1986		21in (53cm)	$2500-up
71	Rabbits	1986		23in (58cm)	$3800-up/pair
72	Bunny	1987		8.5in (22cm)	$750-up
72	(Left) Hedgehog	1987		15in (38cm)	$1300-up
	(Center) Beaver	1987		16in (41cm)	$1200-up
	(Right) Owl	1987		12in (31cm)	$1000-up
73	Monkey	1987		23in (58cm)	$2000-up
73	Pigs	1987		23in (58cm)	$3500-up/pair
74	Cat	1989		20in (51cm)	$1200-up

INDEX